Routledge Revivals

The Life and Teaching of Karl Marx

First published in English in 1921, this work was originally written by renowned Marxist historian Max Beer to commemorate the centenary of Marx's birth. It is a definitive biography, full of interesting personal details and a clear and comprehensive account of Marx's economic and historical doctrines. A special feature of this unique work is the new light thrown on Marx's attitude to the "Dictatorship of the Proletariat" and Bolshevist methods generally.

I0129066

The Life and Teaching of Karl Marx

Max Beer

Translated by
T. C. Partington
&
H. J. Stenning
and revised by the author

Routledge
Taylor & Francis Group

First published in English in 1921

This edition first published in 2011 by Routledge
2 Park Square, Milton Park, Abingdon, Oxon, OX14 4RN

Simultaneously published in the USA and Canada
by Routledge
711 Third Avenue, New York, NY 10017

Routledge is an imprint of the Taylor & Francis Group, an informa business

Publisher's Note
The publisher has gone to great lengths to ensure the quality of this
reprint but points out that some imperfections in the original copies may
be apparent.

Disclaimer
The publisher has made every effort to trace copyright holders and
welcomes correspondence from those they have been unable to contact.

A Library of Congress record exists under LC Control Number: 22018875

ISBN 13: 978-0-415-67633-5 (hbk)
ISBN 13: 978-0-415-67745-5 (pbk)
ISBN 13: 978-0-203-80839-9 (ebk)

THE
LIFE AND TEACHING
OF
KARL MARX

BY
M. BEER
Author of "A History of British Socialism"

TRANSLATED BY T. C. PARTINGTON
AND H. J. STENNING, AND REVISED
BY THE AUTHOR

NATIONAL LABOUR PRESS, LIMITED,
LONDON: 8/9, JOHNSON'S COURT, E.C. 4
MANCHESTER: 30, BLACKFRIARS STREET

First Published in 1921

CONTENTS.

INTRODUCTION.

I. THE SIGNIFICANCE OF MARX.

KARL MARX belongs to the ranks of those philosophical and sociological thinkers who throw potent thought-ferment into the world, and set in motion the masses of mankind. They awaken slumbering doubts and contradictions. They proclaim new modes of thought, new social forms. Their systems may sooner or later become obsolete, and the ruthless march of time may finally overthrow their intellectual edifice; meanwhile, however, they stimulate into activity the minds of countless men, inflame countless human hearts, imprinting on them characteristics which are transmitted to coming generations. This is the grandest and finest work to which any human being can be called. Because these thinkers have lived and worked, their contemporaries and successors think more clearly, feel more intensely, and are richer in knowledge and self-consciousness.

The history of philosophy and of social science is comprised in such systems and generalisations. They are the index to the annals of mankind. None of these systems is complete, none comprehends all human motives and capacities, none exhausts all the forces and currents of human society. They all express only fragmentary truths, which, however, become effective and achieve success because they are shining lights amidst the intellectual confusion of the generation which gives them birth, bringing it to a consciousness of the questions of the time, rendering its further development less difficult, and enabling its strongest spirits to stand erect, with fixity of purpose, in critical periods.

Hegel expresses himself in a similar sense where he remarks : " When the refutation of a philosophy is spoken of, this is usually meant in an abstract negative (completely destructive) sense, so that the confuted philosophy has no longer any validity whatever, and is set aside and done with. If this be so, the study of the history of philosophy must be regarded as a thoroughly depressing business, seeing that this study teaches that every system of philosophy which has arisen in the course of time has found its refutation. But if it is as good as granted that every philosophy has been refuted, yet at the same time it must be also asserted that no philosophy has been refuted, nor ever can be refuted . . . for every philosophical system is to be considered as the presentation of a particular moment or a particular stage in the evolutionary process of the idea. The history of philosophy . . . is not, in its totality, a gallery of the aberrations of the human intellect, but is rather to be compared to a pantheon of deities."

—(" Hegel, Encyclopædia," vol. 1, section 86, note 2.)

What Hegel says here about philosophy is true also of systems of social science, and styles and forms in art. The displacement of one system by another reflects the historical sequence of the various stages of social evolution. The characteristic which is common to all these systems is their vitality.

In spite of their defects and difficulties there surges through them a living spirit from the influence of which contemporaries cannot escape. Opponents may put themselves to endless trouble to contradict such systems, and show up their shortcomings and inconsistencies, and yet, with all their pains, they do not succeed in attaining their object; their logical sapping and mining, their passionate attacks break against the vital spirit which the creative genius has breathed into his work. The deep impression made on us by this vitality is one of the main factors in the formation of our judgments upon scientific and artistic achievements. Mere formal perfection and beauty through which the life of the times does not throb can never create this impression.

Walter Scott, who was often reproached with defects and inconsistencies in the construction of his novels, once made answer with the following anecdote: A French sculptor, who had taken up his abode in Rome, was fond of taking to the Capitol his artistically inclined countrymen who were travelling in Italy, to show them the equestrian statue of Marcus Aurelius, on which occasions he was at pains to demonstrate that the horse was defectively modelled, and did not meet the requirements of anatomy. After one of these criticisms a visitor urged him to prove his case in a concrete form by constructing a horse on correct artistic principles. The critic set to work, and when, after the lapse of a year, his friends were again visiting Rome, exhibited to them his horse. It was anatomically perfect. Proudly he had it brought to the Capitol, in order to compare both productions and so celebrate his triumph. Quite absorbed in his critical comparison, the French sculptor after a while gave way to a burst of genuine artistic feeling, which caused him pathetically to exclaim, " *Et pourtant*

cette bête-là est vivante, et la mienne est morte! "
(And yet that animal is alive, while mine is dead.)

Quite a number of Marxian critics find themselves
in the same position as the hypercritical French
sculptor. Their formal and logically complete
economic doctrines and systems of historical philosophy, provided with pedantically correct details and
definitions, remain dead and ineffective. They do not
put us into contact with the relations of the time,
whereas Marx has bequeathed both to the educated
and the uneducated, to his readers and to non-readers,
a multitude of ideas and expressions relating to social
science, which have become current throughout the
whole world.

In Petrograd and in Tokio, in Berlin and in London,
in Paris and in Pittsburg, people speak of capital and
of the capitalist system, of means of production and
of the class struggle; of Reform and Revolution; of
the Proletariat and of Socialism. The extent of Marx's
influence is shown by the economic explanation of the
world-war, which is even accepted by the most decided
opponents of the materialist conception of history. A
generation after Marx's death, the sovereignty of
Capital shrinks visibly, works' committees and shops'
stewards interfere with the productive processes,
Socialists and Labour men fill the Parliaments,
working men and their representatives rise to or take
by storm the highest position of political power in
States and Empires. Many of their triumphs would
scarcely have received Marx's approval. His theory,
white-hot with indomitable passion, demanded that
the new tables of the Law should be given to men
amidst thunder and lightning. But still the essential
thing is that the proletariat is loosening its bonds, even

if it does not burst them noisily asunder. We find ourselves in the first stages of the evolution of Socialist society. Through whatever forms this evolutionary process may pass in its logical development, this much is certain, that only by active thought on the part of Socialists and by the loyal co-operation of the workers can it be brought to its perfection.

We are already using Hegelian expressions, and must therefore pause here to note briefly Hegel's contribution to the subject. Without a knowledge of this, no one can be in a position to appreciate the important factors in the life and influence of Marx, or even to understand his first intellectual achievements during his student years.

II. THE WORK OF HEGEL.

Until towards the end of the eighteenth century, learned and unlearned, philosophers and philistines, had some such general notions as the following. The world has either been created, or it has existed from eternity. It is either governed by a personal, super-natural god or universal spirit, or it is kept going by nature, like some delicate machine. It exists in accordance with eternal laws, and is perfect, ordained to fulfil some design, and constant. The things and beings which are found in it are divided into kinds, species and classes. All is fixed, constant and eternal. Things and beings are contiguous in space, and succeed one another in time, as they have done ever since time was. It is the same with the incidents and events of the world and of mankind. Such common

proverbs as " There is nothing new under the sun "
and " History repeats itself " are but the popular
expression of this view.

Correlative to this philosophy was Logic, or the
science of the laws of thinking (Greek logos—reason,
word). It taught how men should use their reason,
how they should express themselves reasonably, how
concepts arise (in what manner, for example, the
human understanding arrived at the concepts stone,
tree, animal, man, virtue, vice, etc.); further, how
such concepts are combined into judgments (propositions), and finally, how conclusions are drawn from
these judgments. This logic exhibited the intellectual
processes of the human mind. It was founded by the
Greek philosopher, Aristotle (884 to 822 B.C.), and
remained essentially unaltered until the beginning of
the nineteenth century, in the same way as our whole
conception of the universe remained unchanged. This
science of human intellectual processes was based on
three original laws of thought, which best characterise
it. Just as an examining magistrate looks a prisoner
in the face, and identifies him, so that uncertainty and
contradiction may be avoided, so this logic began by
establishing the identity of the conceptions with which
it was to operate. Consequently, it established as the
first law of thought the Principle of Identity, which
runs as follows : A=A, i.e., each thing, each being, is
like itself ; it possesses an individuality of its own,
peculiar to itself. To put it more clearly, this principle affirms that the earth is the earth, a state is a
state, Capital is Capital, Socialism is Socialism.

From this proceeds the second law of thought, the
Principle of Contradiction. A cannot be A and
not—A. Or following our example given above, the

earth cannot be the earth and a ball of fire; a State cannot be a State and an Anarchy; Capital cannot be Capital and Poverty; Socialism cannot be Socialism and Individualism. Therefore there must be no contradictions, for a thing which contradicts itself is nonsense; where, however, this occurs either in actuality or in thought, it is only an accidental exception to the rule, as it were, or a passing and irregular phenomenon.

From this law of thought follows directly the third, viz., the Principle of the Excluded Middle. A thing is either A or non-A; there is no middle term. Or, according to our example, the earth is either a solid body, or, if it is not solid, it is no earth; there is no middle term. The State is either monarchical, or, if it is not monarchical, it is no State. Capitalism is either oppressive, or altogether not Capitalism. Socialism is either revolutionary, or not Socialism at all; there is no middle term. (Socialism is either reformist, or not Socialism at all; there is no middle term.)

With these three intellectual laws of identity, of contradiction, and of the excluded middle, formal logic begins.

It is at once apparent that this logic operates with rigid, constant, unchanging, dogmatic conceptions, something like geometry, which deals with definitely bounded spatial forms. Such was the rationale of the old world-philosophy.

By the beginning of the nineteenth century a new conception of the world had begun to make its way. The world, as we see it, or get to know it from books, was neither created, nor has it existed from time immemorial, but has developed in the course of uncounted thousands of years, and is still in process of development. It has traversed a whole series of changes, transformations, and catastrophes. The earth was a gaseous mass, then a ball of fire; the species and classes of things and beings which exist on the earth have partly arisen by gradual transition from one sort into another, and partly made their appearance as a result of sudden changes. And in human history it is the same as in nature; the form and significance of the family, of the State, of production, of religion, of law, etc., are subjected to a process of development. All things are in flux, in a state of becoming, of arising and disappearing. There is nothing rigid, constant, unchanging in the Cosmos.

In view of the new conception, the old formal logic could no longer satisfy the intellect; it could not adequately deal with things in a state of evolution. In ever-increasing measure it became impossible for the thinker to work with hard and fast conceptions. From the beginning of the nineteenth century a new logic was sought, and it was G. W. F. Hegel (1770—1831) who made a comprehensive and thoroughly painstaking endeavour to formulate a new logic in accordance with the universal process of evolution. This task appeared to him to be the more urgent, as his whole philosophy aimed at bringing thought and being, reason and the universe, into the closest connection and agreement, dealing with them as inseparable from each other, regarding them as identical, and representing the universe as the gradual embodiment of Reason. " What is reasonable is real; what is real is reasonable." The task of philosophy is to comprehend what is. Every individual is the child of his time. Even philosophy is its time grasped in thought. No individual can overleap his time.

(Pref. to Phil. of Law.) It is evident that, in his way, Hegel was no abstract thinker, divorced from actuality, and speculating at large. Rather he set himself to give material content to the abstract and purely ideal, to make it concrete, in fact. The idea without reality, or reality without the idea, seemed to him unthinkable. Accordingly his logic could not deal merely with the laws of thought, but must at the same time take account of the laws of cosmic evolution. Merely to play with the forms of thought, and to fence with ideas, as the old logicians, especially in the Middle Ages, were wont to do, seemed to him a useless, abstract, unreal operation. He, therefore, created a science of thinking, which formulated not only the laws of thought, but also the laws of evolution, albeit, unfortunately, in a language which offered immense difficulties to his readers.

The essence of his logic is the dialectic.

By dialectic the old Greeks understood the art of discourse and rejoinder, the refutation of an opponent by the destruction of his assertions and proofs, the bringing into relief of the contradictions and antitheses. When examined closely, this art of discussion, in spite of its contradictory and apparently negative (destructive) intellectual work, is seen to be very useful, because, out of the clash of opposing opinions, it brings forth the truth and stimulates to deeper thought. Hegel seized hold of this expression, and named his logical method after it. This is the dialectical method, or the manner of conceiving the things and beings of the universe as in the process of becoming, through the struggle of contradictory elements and their resolution. With its aid, he brings to judgment the three original laws of thought which

have already been alluded to. The principle of
identity is an abstract, incomplete truth, for it
separates a thing from the variety of other things, and
its relations to them. Everybody will see this to be
true. Let us take the proposition : the earth is the
earth. Whoever hears the first three words of this
proposition naturally expects that what is predicated
of the earth should tell him something which distinguishes the earth from other things. Instead of this,
he is offered an empty, hard and fast identity, the
dead husk of an idea. If the principle of identity is
at best only an incomplete truth, the principles of
contradiction and of the excluded middle are complete
untruths. Far from making a thought nonsense,
contradiction is the very thing which unfolds and
develops the thought, and hence, too, the object which
it expresses. It is precisely opposition, or antithesis,
which sets things in motion, which is the mainspring
of evolution, which calls forth and develops the latent
forces and powers of being. Had the earth as a fiery,
gaseous mass remained in that state, without the
contradiction, that is, the cooling and condensation,
taking place, then no life would have appeared on it.
Had the State remained autocratic, and the contradictory principle, middle-class freedom, been absent,
then the life of the State would have become rigid,
and the bloom of culture rendered impossible. Had
Capitalism remained without its proletarian contradiction, then it would have reverted to an industrial
feudalism. It is the contradiction, or the antithesis,
which brings into being the whole kingdom of the
potentialities and gifts of nature and of humanity.
Only when the contradictory begins to reveal itself
does evolution to a higher plane of thought and

existence begin. It is obvious that we are not concerned here with logical contradictions, which usually arise from unclear thinking or from confusion in the presentation of facts; Hegel, and after him Marx, dealt rather with real contradictions, with antitheses and conflicts, as they arise of themselves in the process of evolution of things and conditions.

The thing or the being, against which the contradiction operates, was called by Hegel the Positive, and the contradiction, the antagonistic element, or the antithesis, he called the Negation. As may be seen from our example, this negation is not mere annihilation, not a resolution int nothing, but a clearing away and a building up at the same time; a disappearance and a coming into existence; a movement to a higher stage. Hegel says in this connection : " It has been hitherto one of the rooted prejudices of logic and a commonly accepted belief that the contradiction is not so essential or so inherent a characteristic (in thought and existence) as the identity. Yet in comparison with it the identity is, in truth, but the characteristic of what is simply and directly perceived, of lifeless existence. The contradiction, however, is the source of all movement and life; only in so far as it contains a contradiction can anything have movement, power, and effect."

The part played by the contradiction, the antithesis, or the negation very easily escapes a superficial observer. He sees, indeed, that the world is filled with a variety of things, and that where anything is there is also its opposite; e.g., existence—non-existence, cold—heat, light—darkness, mildness—harshness, pleasure—pain, joy—sorrow, riches—poverty, Capital —Labour, life—death, virtue—vice, Idealism—

Materialism, Romanticism—Classicism, etc., but superficial thought does not realise that it is faced with a world of contradictions and antitheses ; it only knows that the world is full of varied and manifold things. " Only active reason," says Hegel, " reduced the mere multiplicity and diversity of phenomena to antithesis. And only when pushed to this point do the manifold phenomena become active and mutually stimulating, producing the state of negation, which is the very heart-beat of progress and life." Only through their differentiation and unfolding as opposing forces and factors is further progress beyond the antithesis to a higher positive stage made possible. " Where, however," continues Hegel, " the power to develop the contradiction and bring it to a head is lacking, the thing or the being is shattered on the contradiction."—(Hegel, " Science of Logic," Pt. 1, Sec. 2, pp. 66, 69, 70.)

This thought of Hegel's is of extraordinary import-ance for the understanding of Marxism. It is the soul of the Marxian doctrine of the class-struggle, nay, of the whole Marxian system. One may say that Marx is always on the look-out for contradictions within the social development, for wherever the con-tradiction (antithesis—class struggle) shows itself, there begins, according to Marx-Hegel, the progress to a higher plane.*

We have now become familiar with two expressions of the dialectical method, the positive and the nega-tion. We have seen the first two stages of the process of growth in thought and in reality. The process is not yet complete. It still requires a third stage.

* In one of the later chapters the reader will find the series of contradictions discovered by Marx in the evolution of capitalism. Sec. IV., " Outlines of the Economic Doctrine." Chapter 8, " Economic Contradictions."

This third step Hegel called the Negation of the Negation. With the continued operation of the negation, a new thing or being comes into existence.

To revert to our examples : the complete cooling and condensation of the earth's crust : the rise of the middle-class State : the victory of the Proletariat : these things represent the suspension or the setting aside of the Negation ; the contradiction is thus resolved, and a new stage in the process of evolution is reached. The expressions Positive (or affirmation), Negation, and Negation of the Negation, are also known as thesis, antithesis, and synthesis.

In order to understand this more distinctly, and to visualise it, let us consider an egg. It is something positive, but it contains a germ, which, awakening to life, gradually consumes (i.e., negatives) the contents of the egg. This negation is, however, no mere destruction and annihilation ; on the contrary, it results in the germ developing into a living thing. The negation being complete, the chick breaks through the egg shell. This represents the negation of the negation, whereby there has arisen something organically higher than an egg.

This mode of procedure in human thinking and in the operations of nature and history Hegel called the dialectical method, or the dialectical process. It is evident that the dialectic is at the same time a method of investigation and a philosophy. Hegel outlines his dialectic in the following words :

" The only thing which is required for scientific progress, an elementary principle for the understanding of which one should really strive, is the recognition of the logical principle that the negative is just as much a positive, or that the contradictory does not resolve into nothing, into an abstract nothingness, but actually only into the negation of a special content. . . . In so far as the resultant, the negation, is a definite negation, it has a content. It is a new conception, but a higher and richer conception than the preceding one; for it has been enriched by the negation or antithesis of this; it therefore contains it and more than contains it, being indeed the synthetic unity of itself and its contrary. In this way the system of concepts has to be formed—and is to be perfected by a continual and purely intellectual process which is independent of outside influences." —(Hegel, " Science of Logic " (German), Bk. I., Introduction.)

The dialectical process completes itself not only by gradual transitions, but also by leaps. Hegel remarks :

" It has been said that there are no sudden leaps in nature, and it is a common notion that things have their origin through gradual increase or decrease. But there is also such a thing as sudden transformation from quantity into quality. For example, water does not become gradually hard on cooling, becoming first pulpy and ultimately attaining the rigidity of ice, but turns hard at once. If the temperature be lowered to a certain degree, the water is suddenly changed into ice, i.e., the quantity—the number of degrees of temperature—is transformed into quality— a change in the nature of the thing.—(" Logic " (German), Pt. 1, Sec. 1, p. 464, Ed. 1841.)

Marx handled this method with unsurpassed mastery; with its aid he formulated the laws of the evolution of Socialism. In his earliest works, " The Holy Family " (1844) and the " Poverty of

Philosophy " (1847), written when he was formulating his materialist conception of history, as also in his " Capital," it is with the dialectic of Hegel that he investigates these laws.

" Proletariat and Riches (later Marx would have said Capital) are antitheses. As such they constitute a whole; both are manifestations of the world of private property. The question to be considered is the specific position which both occupy in the antithesis. To describe them as two sides of a whole is not a sufficient explanation. Private property as private property, as riches, is compelled to preserve its own existence, and along with it that of its antithesis, the Proletariat. Private property satisfied in itself is the positive side of the antithesis. The Proletariat, on the other hand, is obliged, as Proletariat, to abolish itself, and along with it private property, its conditioned antithesis, which makes it the Proletariat. It is a negative side of the antithesis, the internal source of unrest, the disintegrated and disintegrating Proletariat. . . . Within the antithesis, therefore, the owner of private property is the conservative, and the proletarian is the destructive party. From the former proceeds the action of maintaining the antithesis, from the latter the action of destroying it. From the point of view of its national, economic movement, private property is, of course, continually being driven towards its own dissolution, but only by an unconscious development which is independent of it, and which exists against its will, and is limited by the nature of things; only, that is, by creating the Proletariat as proletariat, poverty conscious of its own physical and spiritual poverty, and demoralised humanity conscious of its own demoralisation and consequently striving against it.

" The Proletariat fulfils the judgment which private property by the creation of the Proletariat suspends over itself, just as it fulfils the judgment which wage-labour suspends over itself in creating alien riches and its own condemnation. If the Proletariat triumphs, it does not thereby become the absolute side of society, for it triumphs only by abolishing itself and its opposite. In this way both the Proletariat and its conditioned opposite, private property, are done away with."*

The dialectical method is again described in a few sentences on pages 420—421 of the third volume of " Capital " (German), where we read : " In so far as the labour process operates merely between man and nature, its simple elements are common to every form of its social development. But any given historical form of this process further develops its material foundations and its social forms. When it has attained a certain degree of maturity the given historical form is cast off and makes room for a higher one. That the moment of such a crisis has arrived is shown as soon as there is a deepening and widening of the contradiction and antithesis between the conditions of distribution, and consequently also the existing historical form of the conditions of production corresponding to them, on the one hand, and the forces of production, productive capacity, and the state of evolution of its agents, on the other. There then arises a conflict between the material development of production and its corresponding social form."

* Marx, in " The Holy Family " (1844), reprinted by Mehring in the " Collected Works or Literary Remains of Marx and Engels," vol. II., p. 132.

But the Hegelian dialectic appears most strikingly in the famous twenty-fourth chapter (sec. 7) of the first volume of " Capital " (German), where the evolution of capitalism from small middle-class ownership through all phases up to the Socialist revolution is comprehensively outlined in bold strokes : " The capitalist method of appropriation, which springs from the capitalist method of production, and therefore capitalist private property, is the first negation of individual private property based on one's own labour. But capitalist production begets with the inevitableness of a natural process its own negation. It is the negation of the negation." Here we have the three stages : the thesis—private property ; the antithesis—capitalism ; the synthesis—common ownership.

Of critical social writers outside Germany it was Proudhon, in particular, who, in his works " What is Property ? " and " Economic Contradictions, or the Philosophy of Poverty " (1840, 1846), attempted to use the Hegelian dialectic. The fact that he gave his chief book the title " Economic Contradictions " shows that Proudhon was largely preoccupied with Hegel. Nevertheless, he did not get below the surface ; he used the Hegelian formulæ quite mechanically, and lacked the conception of an immanent process of development (the forward-impelling force within the social organism).

If we look at the dialectical method as here presented, Hegel might be taken for a materialist thinker. Such a notion would be erroneous. For Hegel is an idealist : the origin and essence of the process of growth is to be sought, according to him, not in material forces, but in the logical idea, reason, the universal spirit, the absolute, or—in its religious

expression—God.   Before Heacre ted the world He
is to be regarded as an Idea, containing within itself
all forms of being, which it develops dialectically.
The idea creates for itself a material embodiment; it
first expresses itself in the objects of inorganic nature;
then in plants, organisms wherein life awakens; then
in animals, in which the Idea attains to the twilight
of reason; finally, in men, where reason rises into
mind and achieves self-consciousness and freedom.
As self-conscious mind it expresses itself in the history
of peoples, in religion, art and philosophy, in human
institutions, in the family and in law, until it realises
itself in the State as its latest and highest object.

According to Hegel, then, the universal Idea
develops into Godhead in proportion as the material
world rises from the inorganic to the organic, and,
finally, to man.   In the mental part of man, the Idea
arrives at self-consciousness and freedom and becomes
God.   In his cosmology, Hegel is a direct descendant
of the German mystics, Sebastion Franck and Jacob
Boehme.   He was in a much higher degree German
than any of the German philosophers since Leibnitz.

The strangest thing, however, is that Germanism,
Protestantism, and the Prussian State appeared to
Hegel as the highest expression of the universal
mind.   Particularly the Prussian State as it existed
before March, 1848, with its repudiation of all middle-
class reforms and liberalism (of any kind), and its
basis of strong governmental force.

There is little purpose in trying to acquire a logical
conception of Hegelian cosmology.   It is not only
idealist, but, as we said, mystical; it is as in-
conceivable to human reason as the biblical;
it is irrational, and lies beyond the sphere of

reason. Making the universe arise out of pure reason, out of the logical idea, developing through the dialectical process with a consciousness of freedom, it yet concludes in unreason and an obstinate determinism. In Liberalism Hegel saw only a simple negation, a purely destructive factor, which disintegrates the State and resolves it into individuals, thus depriving it of all cohesion and organising strength. He blamed Parliamentarism for demanding " that everything should take place through their (the individuals) expressed power and consent. The will of the many overturns the Ministry, and what was the Opposition now takes control, but, so far as it is the Government, the latter finds the many against it. Thus agitation and unrest continue. This collision, this knot, this problem, is what confronts history, a problem which it must resolve at some future time." One would have thought that it was precisely Parliamentarism, with its unrest and agitation, its antitheses and antagonisms, which would have had a special attraction for Hegel, but nevertheless he turned aside from it. How is this to be explained?

Hegel's relation to the Prussian State is to be accounted for by his strong patriotic sentiments. His disposition inclined him strongly to nationalism in politics. In his early manhood he witnessed the complete dissolution of the German Empire, and deeply bewailed the wretchedness of German conditions. He wrote: " Germany is no longer a State; even the wars which Germany waged have not ended in a particularly honourable manner for her. Burgundy, Alsace, Lorraine have been torn away. The Peace of Westphalia has often been alluded to as Germany's Palladium, although by it the complete dismemberment of Germany has only been established more thoroughly than before. The Germans have been grateful to Richelieu, who destroyed their power." On the other hand, the achievements of Prussia in the Seven Years' War, and in the War of Liberation against the French, awoke in him the hope that it was this State which could save Germany. To this thought he gave eloquent and enthusiastic expression in his address at the opening of his Berlin lectures in October, 1818, and also in his lecture on Frederick the Great. Hegel therefore rejected everything which seemed to him to spell a weakening of the Prussia State power. The dialectician was overcome by national feelings.

However, Hegel's place in the history of thought rests, not on his explanations of the creation of the world, nor on his German nationalist politics, but upon the dialectical method. In exploring, by means of this method, the wide expanse of human knowledge, he scattered an astonishing abundance of materialistic and strictly scientific observations and suggestions, and inspired his pupils and readers with a living conception of history, of the development of mankind to self-consciousness and freedom, thus rendering them capable of pushing their studies further, and emancipating themselves from all mysticism. As an example of the materialist tendency of his philosophy, the following references will serve. His " Philosophy of History " contains a whole chapter upon the geographical foundations of universal history. In this chapter he expresses himself—quite contrary to his deification of the State—as follows : " A real State and a real central government only arise when the distinction of classes is already given, when Riches and Poverty have become very great, and such conditions have arisen that a great multitude can no longer satisfy their needs in the way to which they have been accustomed." Or take his explanation of the founding of colonies by the Greeks.

" This projecting of colonies, particularly in the period after the Trojan War until Cyrus, is here a peculiar phenomenon, which may thus be explained : in the individual towns the people had the governing power in their hands, in that they decided the affairs of State in the last resort. In consequence of the long peace, population and development greatly increased, and quickly brought about the accumulation of great riches, which is always accompanied by the phenomenon of great distress and poverty. Industry, in our sense, did not exist at that time, and the land was speedily monopolised. Nevertheless, a section of the poorer classes would not allow themselves to be depressed to the poverty line, for each man felt himself to be a free citizen. The sole resource, therefore, was colonisation."

Or even the following passage, which conceives the philosophical system merely as the result and reflection of the accomplished facts of existence, and therefore rejects all painting of Utopias : " Besides, philosophy comes always too late to say a word as to how the world ought to be. As an idea of the universe, it only arises in the period after reality has completed its formative process and attained its final shape. What this conception teaches is necessarily demonstrated by history, namely, that the ideal appears over against the real only after the consummation of reality, that the ideal reconstructs the same world, comprehended in the substance of reality, in the form of an intellectual realm. A form of life has become old when philosophy paints its grey on grey, and with grey on grey it cannot be rejuvenated but only recognised. The owl of Minerva begins its flight only with the falling twilight."—Preface to the " Philosophy of Law."

No materialist could have said this better : the owl —the symbol of wisdom—only begins her flight in the evening, after the busy activities of the world are over. Thus we have first the universe, and then thought; first existence, and then consciousness.

Hegel himself was therefore an example of his own teaching that contradictory elements are to be found side by side. His mind contained both idealism and realism, but he did not bring them by a process of reasoning to the point of acute contradiction in order to reach a higher plane of thought. And as he regarded it as the task of philosophy to recognise the principle of things, and to follow it out systematically and logically throughout the whole vast domain of reality, and as further, owing to his mystical bent, he asserted the idea to be the ultimate reality, he remained a consistent Idealist.

The Conservatism of Hegel, who was the philosophical representative of the Prussian State, was, however, sadly incompatible with the awakening consciousness of the German middle class, which, in spite of its economic weakness, aspired to a freer State constitution, and greater liberty of action. These aspirations were already somewhat more strongly developed in the larger towns and industrial centres of Prussia and the other German States. The Young Hegelians* championed this middle-class awakening in

* After the death of Hegel differences of opinion arose among his disciples, chiefly with respect to his doctrines of the Deity, immortality and the personality of Christ. One section, the so-called " Right Wing," inclined to orthodoxy on these questions. In opposition to them stood the " Young Hegelians," the progressive " Left Wing." To this section belonged Arnold Ruge, Bruno Bauer, Feuerbach, and Strauss, author of the " Life of Jesus."

the philosophical sphere, just as " Young Germany " (Heine, Boerne, etc.) did in the province of literature.

Just at the time when Marx was still at the university the Young Hegelians took up the fight against the conservative section of Hegel's disciples and the Christian Romanticism of Prussia. The antagonism between the old and the new school made itself felt both in religious philosophy and political literature, but both tendencies were seldom combined in the same persons. David Strauss subjected the Gospels to a candid criticism ; Feuerbach investigated the nature of Christianity and of religion generally, and in this department inverted Hegel's Idealism to Materialism ; Bruno Bauer trained his heavy historical and philosophical artillery on the traditional dogmas concerning the rise of Christianity. Politically, however, they remained at the stage of the freedom of the individual : that is, they were merely moderate Liberals. Nevertheless, there were also less prominent Young Hegelians who were at that time in the Liberal left wing as regards their political opinions, such as Arnold Ruge.

None of the Young Hegelians had, however, used the dialectical method to develop still further the teaching of the Master. Karl Marx, the youngest of the Hegelians, first brought it to a higher stage in social science. He was no longer known to Hegel, who might otherwise have died with a more contented or perhaps even still more perturbed mind. Heinrich Heine, who belonged to the Hegelians in the thirties and forties, relates the following anecdote, which if not true yet excellently illustrates the extraordinary difficulties of the Master's doctrines :—

As Hegel lay dying, his disciples, who had gathered

round him, seeing the furrows deepen on the Master's care-worn countenance, inquired the cause of his grief, and tried to comfort him by reminding him of the large number of admiring disciples and followers he would leave behind. Breathing with difficulty, he replied : " None of my disciples has understood me ; only Michelet has understood me, and," he added with a sigh, " even he has misunderstood me."

The Life and Teaching of Karl Marx

I.

PARENTS AND FRIENDS.

I. Marx's Apprenticeship.

Karl Heinrich Marx first saw the light of day in Treves on May 5, 1818. His father, an enlightened, fine feeling, and philanthropic Jew, was a Jurist who had slowly risen from the humble circumstances of a German Rabbi family and acquired a respectable practice, but who never learnt the art of making money. His mother was a Dutchwoman, and came of a Rabbi family called Pressburg, which, as the name indicates, had emigrated from Pressburg, in Hungary, to Holland, in the seventeenth century. She spoke German very imperfectly. Marx has handed on to us one of her sayings, " If Karl made a lot of Capital, instead of writing a lot about Capital, it would have been much better." The Marxes had several children, of whom Karl alone showed special mental gifts.

In the year 1824 the family embraced Christianity. The baptism of Jews was at that time no longer a rarity. The enlightenment of the last half of the eighteenth century had undermined the dogmatic

beliefs of many cultured Jews, and the succeeding
period of German Christian Romanticism brought a
strengthening and idealising of Christianity and of
national feeling, from which, for practical just as much
as for spiritual reasons. the Jews who had renounced
their own religion could not escape. They were
completely assimilated, felt and thought like the
rest of their Christian and German fellow-citizens.
Marx's father felt himself to be a good Prussian,
and once recommended his son to compose an
ode, in the grand style, on Napoleon's downfall
and Prussia's victory. Karl did not, in truth, follow
his father's advice, but from that time of Christian
enthusiasm and German patriotic sentiment until his
life's end, there remained with him an anti-Jewish
prejudice; the Jew was generally to him either a
usurer or a cadger.

Karl was sent to the grammar school in his native
town, leaving with a highly creditable record. The
school was, however, not the only place where he
developed his mind. During his school years he used
to frequent the house of the Government Privy
Councillor, L. von Westphalen, a highly cultured
Prussian official, whose favourite poets were Homer
and Shakespeare, and who followed attentively the
intellectual tendencies of his time. Although he had
already reached advanced age, he liked to converse
with the precocious youth, and to influence his mental
growth. Marx honoured him as a fatherly friend
" who welcomes every progressive movement with the
enthusiasm and sober judgment of a lover of truth,
and who is a living proof that Idealism is no
imagination, but the truth."—(Dedication of Marx's
doctor thesis.)

After quitting the public school, Marx went to the University of Bonn, in order to study jurisprudence, according to his father's wishes. After a year of the merry life of a student, he removed in the autumn of 1836 to Berlin University, the centre of culture and truth, as Hegel had called it in his Inaugural Lecture (1818). Before his departure for Berlin, he had become secretly engaged to Jenny Von Westphalen, the daughter of his fatherly friend, a woman distinguished alike for beauty, culture, and strength of character.

II. STUDENT.

In Berlin, Marx threw himself into the study of Philosophy, Jurisprudence, History, Geography, Literature, the History of Art, etc. He had a Faustlike thirst for truth, and his appetite for work was insatiable; in these matters only superlatives can be used to describe Marx. In one of his poems dating from this period, he says of himself :

" Ne'er can I perform in calmness
    What has seized my soul with might,
But must strive and struggle onward
    In a ceaseless, restless flight.

All divine, enhancing graces
    Would I make of life a part;
Penetrate the realms of science,
    Grasp the joys of Song and Art."

Giving up all social intercourse, he worked night and day, making abstracts of what he read, translating from Greek and Latin, working at philosophical systems, setting down a considerable number of his own thoughts, and drafting outlines of philosophy or jurisprudence, as well as writing three volumes of poems. The year 1837 marks one of the critical periods of Marx's intellectual development; it was a time of vacillation and ferment and of internal struggle, at the end of which he found refuge in the Hegelian dialectics. In so doing he turned his back on the abstract idealism of Kant and Fichte, and made the first step towards reality; and indeed at that time Marx firmly believed that Hegel actually stood for reality. In a somewhat lengthy letter dated November 10, 1837, a truly human document, Marx gives his father an account of his intense activity during that remarkable period, comprising his first two terms at the University of Berlin, when he was still so very young :

" DEAR FATHER,

" There are times which are landmarks in our lives; and they not only mark off a phase that has passed, but, at the same time, point out clearly our new direction. At such turning points we feel impelled to make a critical survey of the past and the present, so as to attain to a clear knowledge of our actual position. Nay, mankind itself, as all history shows, loves to indulge in this retrospection and contemplation, and thereby often appears to be going backward or standing still, when after all it has only thrown itself back in its armchair, the better to apprehend itself, to grasp its own doings, and to penetrate into the workings of the spirit.

" The individual, however, becomes lyrical at such times; for every metamorphosis is in part an elegy on the past and in part the prologue of a great new poem that is striving for permanent expression in a chaos of resplendent but fleeting colours. Be that as it may, we would fain set up a monument to our past experiences that they may regain in memory the significance which they have lost in the active affairs of life : and what more fitting way can we find of doing that than by bringing them and laying them before the hearts of our parents !

" And so now, when I take stock of the year which I have just spent here, and in so doing answer your very welcome letter from Ems, let me consider my position, in the same way as I look on life altogether, as the embodiment of a spiritual force that seeks expression in every direction : in science, in art, and in one's own personality. . . . On my arrival in Berlin I broke off all my former connections, paid visits rarely and unwillingly, and sought to bury myself in science and art. . . In accordance with my ideas at the time, poetry must of necessity be my first concern, or at least the most agreeable of my pursuits, and the one for which I most cared ; but, as might be expected from my disposition and the whole trend of my development, it was purely idealistic. Next I had to study jurisprudence, and above all I felt a strong impulse to grapple with philosophy. Both studies, however, were so interwoven that on the one hand I worked through the Jurist's Heineccius and Thibaut and the Sources docilely and quite uncritically, translating, for instance, the first two books of the Pandects of Justinian, while on the other hand I attempted to evolve a philosophy of law in the sphere of jurisprudence. By way of introduction I laid down a few metaphysical principles, and carried this unfortunate work as far as Public Rights, in all about 300 sheets.

" In this, however, more than in anything else, the conflict between what is and what ought to be, which is peculiar to Idealism, made itself disagreeably prominent. In the first place there was what I had so graciously christened the Metaphysics of Law, i.e., first principles, reflections, definitions, standing aloof from all established jurisprudence and from every actual form of legal practice. Then the unscientific form of mathematical dogmatism in which there is so much beating about the bush, so much diffuse argumentation without any fruitful development or vital creation, hindered me from the outset from arriving at the Truth. A triangle may be constructed and reasoned about by the mathematician; it is a mere spatial concept and does not of itself undergo any further evolution; it must be brought in conjunction with something else, when it requires other properties, and thus by placing the same thing in various relationships we are enabled to deduce new relationships and new truths. Whereas in the concrete expression of the mental life as we have it in Law, in the State, in Nature, and in the whole of philosophy, the object of our study must be considered in its development. . . The individual's reason must proceed with its self-contradiction until it discovers its own unity."

In this we perceive the first trace of the Hegelian dialectic in Marx. We see rigid geometrical forms contrasted with the continually evolving organism, with social forms and human institutions. Marx had put up a stout resistance against the influence of the Hegelian philosophy; nay, he had even hated it and had made mighty efforts to cling faithfully to his idealism, but in the end he, too, must fall under the spell of the idea of evolution, in the form which it then assumed in Hegelian speculation in Germany.

Marx then goes on to speak of his legal studies as well as of his poems, and thus continues :

" As a result of these various activities I passed many sleepless nights during my first term, engaged in many battles, and had to endure much mental and physical excitement; and at the end of it all I found myself not very much better off, having in the meanwhile neglected nature, art and society, and spurned pleasure : such, indeed, was the comment which my body seemed to make. My doctor advised me to try the country, and so, having for the first time passed through the whole length of the city, I found myself before the gate on the Stralau Road. . . . From the idealism which I had cherished so long I fell to seeking the ideal in reality itself. Whereas before the gods had dwelt above the earth, they had now become its very centre.

" I had read fragments of Hegel's philosophy, the strange, rugged melody of which had not pleased me. Once again I wished to dive into the depths of the sea, this time with the resolute intention of finding a spiritual nature just as essential, concrete, and perfect as the physical, and instead of indulging in intellectual gymnastics, bringing up pure pearls into the sunlight.

" I wrote about 24 sheets of a dialogue entitled
' Cleantes or on the Source and Inevitable Development of Philosophy.' In this, art and science, which
had hitherto been kept asunder, were to some extent
blended, and bold adventurer that I was, I even set
about the task of evolving a philosophical, dialectical exposition of the nature of the Deity as it is
manifested in a pure concept, in religion, in nature,
and in history.   My last thesis was the beginning
of the Hegelian system; and this work, in course of
which I had to make some acquaintance with science,
Schelling and history, and which had occasioned me
an infinite amount of hard thinking, delivers me like
a faithless siren into the hands of the enemy. . . .

" Upset by Jenny's illness and by the fruitless-
ness and utter failure of my intellectual labours, and
torn with vexation at having to make into my idol
a view which I had hated, I fell ill, as I have
already told you in a previous letter.   On my
recovery I burnt all my poems and material for
projected short stories in the vain belief that I could
give all that up; and, to be sure, so far I have not
given cause to gainsay it.

" During my illness I had made acquaintance with
Hegel from beginning to end, as also with most of
his disciples.   Through frequent meetings with
friends in Stralau I got an introduction into a
Graduates' Club, in which were a number of pro-
fessors and Dr. Rutenberg, the closest of my Berlin
friends.   In the discussions that took place many
conflicting views were put forward, and more and
more securely did I get involved in the meshes of
the new philosophy which I had sought to escape;
but everything articulate in me was put to silence,

a veritable ironical rage fell upon me, as well it might after so much negation."—(" Neue Zeit," 16th year, Vol. I., No. 1.)

His father was anything but pleased with this letter. He reproached Karl with the aimless and discursive way in which he worked. He had expected that these Berlin studies would lead to something more than breeding monstrosities and destroying them again. He believed that Karl would, before everything else, have considered his future career, that he would have devoted all his attention to the lectures in his course, that he would have cultivated the acquaintance of people in authority, that he would have been economical, and that he would have avoided all philosophical extravagances. He refers him to the example of his fellow students who attend their lectures regularly and have an eye to their future :

" Indeed these young men sleep quite peacefully except when they now and then devote the whole or part of a night to pleasure, whereas my clever and gifted son Karl passes wretched sleepless nights, wearying body and mind with cheerless study, forbearing all pleasures with the sole object of applying himself to abstruse studies : but what he builds to-day he destroys again to-morrow, and in the end he finds that he has destroyed what he already had, without having gained anything from other people. At last the body begins to ail and the mind gets confused, whilst these ordinary folks steal along in easy marches, and attain their goal if not better at least more comfortably than those who contemn youthful pleasures and undermine their health in order to snatch at the ghost of erudition, which they could probably have exorcised more successfully in an hour spent in the society of competent men—with social enjoyment into the bargain ! "

In spite of his unbounded love for his father, Marx could not deviate from the path which he had chosen. Those deeper natures who, after having lost their religious beliefs, have the good fortune to attain to a philosophical or scientific conception of the universe, do not easily shrink from a conflict between filial affection and loyalty to new convictions. Nor was Marx allured by the prospects of a distinguished official career. Indeed his fighting temperament would never have admitted of that. He wrote the lines :

> Therefore let us, all things daring,
>   Never from our task recede ;
> Never sink in sullen silence,
>   Paralysed in will and deed.

> Let us not in base subjection
>   Brood away our fearful life,
> When with deed and aspiration
>   We might enter in the strife.

His stay in Stralau had the most beneficial effects on his health. He worked strenuously at his newly-acquired philosophical convictions, and for this his relations with the members of the Graduates' Club stood him in good stead, more especially his acquaintance with Bruno Bauer, a lecturer in theology, and Friedrich Köppen, a master in a grammar school, who in spite of difference of age and position treated him as an equal. Marx gave up all thought of an official career, and looked forward to obtaining a lectureship in some university or other. His father reconciled himself to the new studies and strivings of his son; he was, however, not destined to rejoice at Karl's subsequent achievements. After a short illness he died in May, 1838, at the age of fifty-six.

Marx then gave up altogether the study of jurisprudence, and worked all the more assiduously at the perfecting of his philosophical knowledge, preparing himself for his degree examination in order—at the instigation of Bruno Bauer—to get himself admitted as quickly as possible as lecturer in philosophy at the University of Bonn. Bauer himself expected to be made Professor of Theology in Bonn after having served as lecturer in Berlin from 1834 to 1839 and in Bonn during the year 1840. Marx wrote a thesis on the Natural Philosophies of Democritus and Epicurus, and in 1841 the degree of Doctor of Philosophy was conferred on him at Jena. He then went over to his friend Bauer in Bonn, where he thought to begin his career as lecturer. Meanwhile his hopes had disappeared. Prussian universities were at that time no places for free inquirers. It was not even possible for Bauer to obtain a professorship; still less could Marx, who was much more violent in the expression of his opinions, reckon on an academic career. His only way out of this blind alley was free-lance journalism, and for this an opportunity soon presented itself.

III. BEGINNINGS OF PUBLIC LIFE.

Marx made his entry into public life with a thorough philosophical training and with an irrestrainable impulse to enter into the struggle for the spiritual freedom of Germany. By spiritual freedom he understood first and foremost freedom in religion and liberalism in politics. He was, too, perfectly clear as to the instrument to be used : it was criticism. The positive and rigid having become ineffectual and unreasonable, is to fall before the weapon of criticism and so make room for a living stream of thought and being, or as Marx himself expressed it in 1844, " to make the petrified conditions dance by singing to them their own tune." Their own tune is, of course, the dialectic. Criticism, generally speaking, was the weapon of the Young Hegelians. Criticism is negation, sweeping away existing conditions and prevailing dogmas to make a clear path for life. Not the setting up of new principles or new dogmas, but the clearing away of the old dogmas is the task of the Young Hegelians. For if dialectic be rightly understood, criticism or negation is the best positive work. Criticism finds expression, above all, in polemics, in the literal meaning of waging war—ruthless war— against the unreal for the purpose of shaking up one's contemporaries.

After Marx had given up all hope of an academic career, the only field of labour that remained open to him was, as we have already said, that of journalism. His material circumstances compelled him, moreover, to consider the question of an independent livelihood. Just about this time the Liberals in the Rhine provinces took up a scheme for the foundation of a newspaper, the object of which was to prepare the way for conditions of greater freedom. The necessary money was soon procured. Significantly enough, Young Hegelians were kept in view for editors and contributors. On the first of January, 1842, the first number of the *Rheinische Zeitung* was published at Cologne. The editor was Dr. Rutenberg, who had formed an intimate friendship with Marx at the time the latter was attending the University of Berlin; and so Marx, then in Bonn, was also invited to contribute. He accepted the invitation, and his essays brought him to the notice of Arnold Ruge, who likewise invited him to take part in his literary undertakings in conjunction with Feuerbach, Bauer, Moses Hess, and others. Marx's essays were greatly appreciated, too, by the readers of the *Rheinische Zeitung*, so that in October, 1842, on the retirement of Rutenberg, he was called to the editorial chair of that journal. In his new position he had to deal with a series of economic and political questions which, no doubt, with a less conscientious editor would have occasioned little hard thinking, but which for Marx showed the need of a thorough study of political economy and Socialism. In October, 1842, a congress of French and German intellectuals was held in Strasburg, and amongst other things French Socialist theories were discussed. Likewise in the Rhine provinces arose questions concerning landed property and taxes, which had to be dealt with from the editorial chair, questions which were not to be answered by a purely philosophical knowledge. Besides, the censorship made the way hard for a paper conducted with such critical acumen, and did not allow the editor to fulfil his real mission. In the preface to "The Critique of Political Economy" (1859) Marx gives a short sketch of his editorial life :

" As editor of the *Rheinische Zeitung*, in 1842 and 1843 I came up, for the first time, against the difficulty of having to take part in the controversy over so-called material interests. The proceedings of the Diet of the Rhine provinces with regard to wood stealing and parcelling out of landed property, and their action towards the farmers of the Moselle districts, and lastly debates on Free Trade and Protection, gave the first stimulus to my investigation of economic questions. On the other hand, an echo of French Socialism and Communism, feebly philosophical in tone, had at that time made itself heard in the columns of the *Rheinische Zeitung*. I declared myself against superficiality, confessing, however, at the same time that the studies I had made so far did not allow me to venture any judgment of my own on the significance of the French tendencies. I readily took advantage of the illusion cherished by the directors of the *Rheinische Zeitung*, who believed they could reverse the death sentence passed on that journal as a result of weak management, in order to withdraw from the public platform into my study."

And so the intellectual need which he felt of studying economics and Socialism, as well as his thirst for free, unfettered activity, resulted in Marx's retirement from his post as editor, although he was about to enter upon married life and had to make provision for his own household. But he was from the beginning determined to subordinate his material existence to his spiritual aspirations.

II.

THE FORMATIVE PERIOD OF MARXISM.

I. THE FRANCO-GERMAN YEAR BOOKS.

BETWEEN the years 1843 and 1844 we have the second and probably the most important critical period in the intellectual development of Marx. In 1837 he had become a disciple of Hegel, into whose philosophy he penetrated deeper and deeper during the two years which ensued. Between 1843 and 1844 he became a Socialist, and in the following two years he laid the foundations of those social and historical doctrines associated with his name. Of the way he came to be a Socialist and by what studies he was led to Socialism, we know nothing. All that can be said is that in the summer of 1843 he must have pursued the reading of French Socialist literature just as assiduously as he did the study of Hegel in 1837. In his letters to Arnold Ruge, written about 1843, and printed in the Franco-German Year Books, we find a few passages which bear witness to his sudden turn-over. In a letter from Cologne (May, 1843) he remarks : " This system of acquisition and commercialism, of possession and of the exploitation of mankind, is leading even more swiftly than the increase of population to a breach within the present society, which the old system cannot heal, because indeed it has not the power either to heal or create, but only to exist and enjoy."

That is still in the sentimental vein, and anything but dialectical criticism. In the following few months, however, he made surprisingly rapid progress towards the fundamental ideas of that conception of history and society, which later on came to be known as Marxism, and which he almost built up into a complete system during those restless years of exuberant creative activity, 1845—46. In a letter from Kreuznach, dated September, 1848, he shows already an acquaintance with Fourier, Proudhon, Cabet, Weitling, etc., and sees his task not in the setting up of Utopias but in the criticism of political and social conditions, " in interpreting the struggles and aspirations of the age." And by the winter of 1848 he has already advanced so much as to be able to write the introduction to the criticism of Hegel's " Philosophy of Law," which is one of the boldest and most brilliant of his essays. He deals with the question of a German revolution, and asks which is the class that could bring about the liberation of Germany. His answer is that the positive conditions for the German revolution and liberation are to be sought " in the formation of a class in chains, a class which finds itself in bourgeois society, but which is not of it, of an order which shall break up all orders. The product of this dissolution of society reduced to a special order is the proletariat. The proletariat arises in Germany only with the beginning of the industrial movement; for it is not poverty resulting from natural circumstances but poverty artificially created, not the masses who are held down by the weight of the social system but the multitude arising from the acute break-up of society—especially of the middle class—which gives rise to the proletariat. When the proletariat proclaims the dissolution of the existing order of things, it is merely announcing the secret of its own existence, for it is in itself the virtual dissolution of this order of things. When the proletariat desires the negation of private property, it is merely elevating to a general principle of society what it already involuntarily embodies in itself as the negative product of society."

Marx wrote this in Paris, whither he had removed with his young wife in October, 1843, in order to take up the editorship of the Franco-German Year Books founded by Arnold Ruge. In a letter addressed to Ruge from Kreuznach in September, 1843, Marx summed up the program of this periodical as follows : " If the shaping of the future and its final reconstruction is not our business, yet it is all the more evident what we have to accomplish with our joint efforts, I mean the fearless criticism of all existing institutions— fearless in the sense that it does not flinch either from its logical consequences or from the conflict with the powers that be. I am therefore not with those who would have us set up the standard of dogmatism ; far from it ; we should rather try to give what help we can to those who are involved in dogma, so that they may realise the implications of their own principles. So, for example, Communism as taught by Cabet, Dezamy, Weitling, and others is a dogmatic abstraction. . . . Moreover, we want to work upon our contemporaries, and particularly on our German contemporaries. The question is : How is that to be done ? Two factors cannot be ignored. In the first place religion, in the second place politics, are the two things which claim most attention in the Germany of to-day. . . . As far as everyday life is concerned, the political State, even where it has not been consciously perfected through Socialist demands, exactly

fulfils, in all its modern forms, the demands of reason.
Nor does it stop there. It presupposes reason everywhere as having been realised. But in so doing it
lands itself everywhere in the contradiction between
its ideal purpose and its real achievements. Out of
this conflict, therefore, of the political State with itself
social truth is evolved."

Without a doubt, the Hegelian conception of the
State as the embodiment of reason and morality did
not accord well with the constitution and the working
of the actual State. And Marx goes on to remark
that in its history the political State is the expression
of the struggles, the needs, and the realities of society.
It is not true, then, as the French and English
Utopians have thought, that the treatment of political
questions is beneath the dignity of Socialists. Rather
is it work of this kind which leads into party conflict
and away from the abstract theory. " We do not
then proclaim to the world in doctrinaire fashion any
new principle : ' This is the truth, bow down before
it ! ' We do not say : ' Refrain from strife, it is
foolishness ! ' We only make clear to men for what
they are really struggling, and to the consciousness of
this they must come whether they will or not."

That is conceived in a thoroughly dialectical vein.
The thinker propounds no fresh problems, brings
forward no abstract dogmas, but awakens an understanding for the growth of the future out of the past,
inspiring the political and social warriors with the
consciousness of their own action.

II. FRIENDSHIP WITH FRIEDRICH ENGELS.

Of the Franco-German Year Books only one number appeared (Spring, 1844). Alongside Marx's contributions (an Introduction to the criticism of Hegel's " Philosophy of Jurisprudence and a review of Bauer's book on the Jewish Question) the volume contains a comprehensive treatise, " Outlines for a Criticism of Political Economy," from the pen of Friedrich Engels (born in Barmen, 1820; died in London, 1895), who was then living in Manchester. In September, 1844, Engels went to visit Marx in Paris. This visit was the beginning of the lifelong intimate friendship between the two men, who without a close collaboration would not have achieved what they did.

Marx was a highly-gifted theorist, a master in the realm of thought, but he was quite unpractical in the affairs of everyday life. Had he enjoyed a regular income throughout life, he would probably have attained his end even without the help of Engels. On the other hand, Engels was an exceedingly able, energetic, and highly-cultured man, eminently practical and successful in everything he undertook, but not endowed with that speculative temperament which surmounts intellectual crises and opens out new horizons. But for his intellectual association with Marx he would, in all probability, have remained little more than a Moses Hess. Marx was never a Utopian ; the complete saturation of his mind with Hegelian dialectics made him immune to all eternal truths and final social forms. On the contrary, up to 1844 Engels was a Utopian—until Marx explained to him the meaning of political and social conflicts, the basis and the motive force, the statics and dynamics of the history of civilised mankind. Engels' " Criticism of Political Economy " is very noteworthy performance for a youth of twenty-three engaged in commerce, but it does not rise above the level of the writings of Owen, Fourier, and Proudhon. Engels' contributions to Owen's " New Moral World " (1843—44) are indeed more philosophical than the other articles by Owenites, but as far as matter goes, there is no perceptible difference between them. " The System of Economic Contradictions," on which Proudhon was working when Engels published his " Outlines," is couched, as far as the critical side is concerned, in the same strain of thought as we find in Engels. Both sought to expose the contradictions of the middle-class economic system, not in order to discover in them the source of the progress of society, but to condemn them in the name of justice. Whereas the Owenites considered their system as perfect, Proudhon and Engels had, independently of one another, striven to free themselves from the Socialist Utopias. Proudhon became a peaceful Anarchist and found salvation in the scheme of autonomous economic groups, which should carry on an exchange of labour equivalents with one another. Engels, on the other hand, found a solution of his difficulties in Marx, whom he rewarded with a lifelong friendship and devotion, which proved to be Marx's salvation. Without Engels' literary and financial help, Marx, with his unpractical, helpless, and, at the same time, proud and uncompromising disposition, would most probably have perished in exile.

III. CONTROVERSIES WITH BAUER AND RUGE.

After the Franco-German Year Books had been
discontinued, Marx, recognising the importance of
economics, studied English and French systems of
political economy with still greater zeal than before,
and continued his studies in Socialism and history with
remarkable steadiness of purpose. No longer now did
he show signs of hesitation or wavering ; he knew
exactly what he wanted. He had left behind him that
period of ideological speculation when he was still a
disciple of Hegel, and he was impelled, as in the
autumn of 1887, to envisage, from his new standpoint,
the past and the future. He takes such a survey in
" The Holy Family," which had its genesis in the
autumn of 1844, and to which Engels also furnished
a slight contribution. It is a settling of accounts with
his former friend and master, Bruno Bauer, and his
brother Edgar, who had not been able to break away
from Hegel. The aim of the book was to force the
Young Hegelians into the path of social criticism, to
urge them forward and prevent them from falling into
stereotyped and abstract ways of thinking. It is not
easy reading. In it Marx has compressed the knowledge he then had of philosophy, history, economics,
and Socialism in concentrated and sharply-cut form.
Besides the excellent sketch of English and French
materialism, which among other things discloses in a
few short but pregnant sentences the connection
between this and English and French Socialism, " The
Holy Family " contains the germs of the materialistic
conception of history as well as the first attempt to
give a social revolutionary interpretation to the class
struggle between Capital and Labour. In the Intro-

duction to the present book a quotation from " The Holy Family " has been given. Speaking against Bauer's conception of history, Marx says : " Or can he believe that he has arrived even at the beginning of a knowledge of historical reality so long as he excludes science and industry from the historical movements? Or does he really think that he can understand any period without having studied, for example, the industries of that period, the immediate means of production of life itself? . . . In the same way as he separated thought from the senses, the soul from the body, and himself from the world, so he separates history from science and industry, and he does not see the birthplace of history in coarse, material production upon earth but in the nebulous constructions in the heavens."—(" Posthumous Works," Vol. II., pp. 259-60.)

Bruno Bauer, who believed in the world-swaying might of the idea, but would not concede that the masses had any power whatever, wrote : " All the great movements of history up to this time were therefore doomed to failure and could not have lasting success, because the masses had taken an interest in them and inspired them—or they must come to a lamentable conclusion because the underlying idea was of such a nature that a superficial apprehension of it must suffice, that is to say, it must reckon on the approval of the masses."

Marx's answer to this was that " the great historical movements had been always determined by mass interests, and only in so far as they represented these interests could the ideas prevail in these movements ; otherwise the ideas might indeed stir up enthusiasm, but they could not achieve any results. The idea always fell into disrepute in so far as it differed from the interest. On the other hand, it is easy to understand that, when it makes its first appearance on the world-stage, every mass interest working itself out in history far exceeds, as an idea or in its presentation, its actual limits and identifies itself purely and simply with the interest of humanity. Thus the idea of the French Revolution not only took hold of the middle classes, in whose interest it manifested itself in great movements, but it also aroused enthusiasm in the labouring masses, for whose conditions of existence it could do nothing. As history has shown, then, ideas have only had effective results in so far as they corresponded to class interests. The enthusiasm, to which such ideas gave birth, arose from the illusion that these ideas signified the liberation of mankind in general.—(" Posthumous Works," Vol. II., pp. 181-8.)

In August, 1844, Marx published under the title " Marginal Notes " in the Paris *Vorwärts* a lengthy polemic against Ruge, which is a defence of Socialism and revolution and takes the part of the German proletariat against Ruge. " As regards the stage of culture or the capacity for culture of the German workers, let me refer to Weitling's clever writings, which in their theoretical aspect often surpass those of Proudhon, however much they may fall behind them in execution. Where would the middle classes, their scholars and philosophers included, be able to show a work like Weitling's ' Guarantees of Peace and Concord ' bearing on the question of emancipation ? If one compares the insipid, spiritless mediocrity of German political literature with this unconstrained and brilliant literary début of the German workers, if one compares these gigantic baby shoes of the proletariat with the dwarfishness of the worn-out political shoes of the German middle classes, one can only prophesy an athletic stature for the German Cinderella. One must admit that the German proletariat is the philosopher of the European proletariat, just as the English proletariat is its political economist and the French proletariat its politician. One must admit that Germany is destined to play just as classic a rôle in the social revolution as it is incompetent to play one in the political. For, as the impotence of the German middle classes is the political impotence of Germany, so the capacity of the German proletariat—even leaving out of account German philosophy—is the social capacity of Germany."

At that time (1844) Marx had already begun to mix among the German working classes resident in Paris, who clung to the various Socialist and Anarchist doctrines which then held sway, and he sought to influence them according to his own ideas. With Heine, too, who at that time was coquetting with Communism, he carried on a sprightly and not unfruitful intercourse. He likewise came into frequent contact with Proudhon, whom he endeavoured to make familiar with Hegelian philosophy. Already in his first work, " What is Property ? " (1840) Proudhon had played with Hegelian formulæ, and Marx probably believed that he could win him over to Socialism. Proudhon, who, like the German Weitling, sprang from the proletariat, ushered in his activity as a social theorist with the above-mentioned work, which had a stimulating effect on Marx and on German Socialists in general, all the more so as Proudhon manifested some acquaintance with classical German philosophy. In this book (" What is Property ? "

German edition, 1844, p. 289) he sums up the whole matter as follows : " Expressing this according to the Hegelian formula, I should say that Communism, the first kind, the first determination of social life, is the first link in social evolution, the *thesis*; property is the antagonistic principle, the *antithesis*; if only we can get the third factor, the *synthesis*, the question is solved. This synthesis comes about only through the cancelling of the thesis by the antithesis; one must therefore in the last instance examine its characteristics, discard what is anti-social, and in the union of the remaining two is then seen the real kind of human social life."

That was indeed a superficial conception of Hegelian dialectics, for what Proudhon wanted to find was not a synthesis but a combination; still for a French working man it was a smart performance to have manipulated German philosophical formulæ, and would justify the most sanguine hopes. Marx did not want to let this opportunity slip, and in " debates both late and long " he discussed Hegelian philosophy with Proudhon.—(Marx : " The Poverty of Philosophy," German edition, Stuttgart, 1885, p. 29.)

In the midst of this activity, however, Marx and other German contributors to the Paris *Vorwärts* were expelled from France in January, 1845, at the instigation of the Prussian Government. Marx packed up his traps and left for Brussels, where he lived, with short interruptions, until the outbreak of the European Revolution in February, 1848. During his sojourn in Brussels his time was occupied mainly with economic studies, for which Engels placed his library of works on political economy at his disposal. Marx embodied the result of these studies in the criticism directed

against Proudhon in his " Misère de la Philosophie "
(Poverty of Philosophy), published in 1847.

IV. CONTROVERSY WITH PROUDHON.

Marx's " Misère de la Philosophie " indicates the
culmination of the first phase of his creative work.
In this critical review he makes his position clear with
respect not only to Proudhon but to Utopian Socialism
in general. It marks also the turning point in the
studies of Marx : English political economy occupied
henceforth the place which German philosophy had
held. The anti-Proudhon controversy is therefore
worthy of a fuller treatment.

Pierre Joseph Proudhon (b. 1809 in Besançon, d.
1865 in Paris) was one of the most gifted and most
distinguished of social philosophers which the modern
proletariat has produced. He was originally a com-
positor, like his similarly minded English contem-
porary, John Francis Bray, the author of " Labour's
Wrongs," published in 1839, but he had a much
greater inclination for study and a more fruitful
literary talent. He managed to acquire, self-taught,
a knowledge of the classical languages, of mathematics
and of science, read assiduously but indiscriminately
works on economics, philosophy, and history, and
applied himself to social criticism. It is rare for a
working man in the West of Europe to feel impelled
to make an acquaintance with Kant, Hegel, and
Feuerbach as Proudhon did through French transla-
tions and through intercourse with German scholars
in Paris. He possessed the noble ambition of blending

French sprightliness with German thoroughness. But self-instruction failed to give him that intellectual training which is more valuable than knowledge, and which alone gives the power to order and to utilise the information acquired, as well as to submit one's own work to self-criticism. The value of a systematic education does not consist in the main in the acquisition of knowledge but in the training of our intellectual faculties as instruments of inquiry and apprehension, of methodical thinking and of sound judgment, to enable us to find our bearings more easily in the chaos of phenomena, experiences, and ideas. A self-taught man may no doubt attain to this degree of culture, but only if his first attempts at independent creative work are submitted to a strict but kindly criticism, which makes him discipline his thoughts. This was not the case with Proudhon; he lacked mental self-discipline. His first work, " What is Property ? " (1840) brought him immediate recognition and strengthened him in his high opinion of his knowledge and his powers, even to the point of making him conceited. When, for example, the French historian, Michelet, disapproved of his dictum, " Property is robbery," Proudhon replied, " Not twice in a thousand years does one come across a pronouncement like that."—(" Economic Contradictions," Leipzig, 1847, Vol. II., p. 301.) And yet the idea is as old as Communism itself. Besides all this, the vivacity and exuberance of language for which Proudhon was noted easily blinded him to the shortcomings of his intellectual culture. Thus it often happened that he rediscovered ideas of his predecessors and published them to the world with naïve pride. Through page after page of argument he holds the

reader in expectation of the explanation, which he is
about to give, of the nature of value, which he rightly
characterises as the "corner-stone of political
economy." At last he will disclose the secret : " It
is time to make ourselves acquainted with this power.
This power . . . is *labour*." His main work, " The
System of Economic Contradictions," swarms with
philosophical formulæ and expressions like thesis,
antithesis, antinomies, synthesis, dialectics, induction,
syllogisms, etc., as also with Latin, Greek, and
Hebrew etymologies ; it often wanders into irrelevant
theological and philosophical digressions and side
issues, not so much with the intention of parading
the author's knowledge as from his lack of intellectual
discipline and insufficient command of his material.
The work in question was to combine German philosophy with French and English political economy,
and its author believed that it would secure for him
before everything else the admiration of the German
Socialists, especially of Marx. He drew the latter's
attention to it by letter, and awaited his " rigorous
criticism." The criticism came in " Misère de la
Philosophie " (Brussels, 1847), but it could no longer
fulfil its purpose, as the fundamental difference between the two men had already widened to a gulf
that could not be bridged. Marx had almost completed his materialistic, logical, and revolutionary
Socialism, Proudhon had laid the foundations of his
peaceful Anarchism with its federative economic
basis. With his searching analysis, his systematised
knowledge, and his great indignation at the presump-
tuous attacks on every Socialist school and leader,
Marx sat in judgment upon Proudhon, exposing him
as a dilettante in philosophy and economics, and at

the same time sketching in outline his own conception of history and economics.

Marx's verdict is damning, yet one cannot but acknowledge that Proudhon, in spite of his obvious insufficiency, had endeavoured, honestly and zealously, to extricate himself from Capitalism as well as from Utopianism, and to outline a scheme for an economic order, in which men, such as he had found them, might lead a free, industrious, and righteous life. The task which Proudhon had set himself was the same as that which engaged the attention of Marx, the criticism of political economy and of the sentimental Utopian Socialism. That is the key-note of Proudhon's system, and it is sounded in almost every chapter. He lacked, however, the requisite knowledge and the historical sense which alone could have made him equal to his task. The whole of his criticism consists virtually in the complaint that riches and poverty accumulate side by side, and that the economic categories—use value, exchange value, division of labour, competition, monopoly, machinery, property, ground rent, credit, tax, etc.—manifest contradictions. Proudhon's special problem was the following : " The workers of any country produce yearly goods to the value, let us say, of 20 milliards. But if the workers, as consumers, wish to buy back these goods they have to pay 25 milliards. The workers are thus cheated out of a fifth. That is a terrible contradiction."— (" What is Property ? " Chap. IV. ; " Economic Contradictions," Vol. I., pp. 292-93.) This statement of the problem shows that Proudhon had no inkling of the essential features of the question of value, in spite of the fact that he cites Adam Smith, David Ricardo, etc., whom he must therefore have read.

Had he really understood these economists and taken up his critical attitude towards them from the standpoint of justice, he would have stated the problem somewhat as follows : The workers of any country produce yearly goods to the value, say, of 20 milliards. For their work, however, they receive as wages a quantity of goods of the value of only 10 or 12 milliards. Is that just? " Only this way of stating the question could possibly have revealed to him the nature of wages, of value, of profit, of capital and its contradictions. Proudhon sees the perpetration of fraud or robbery in the sphere of exchange and not in that of production, and he does not ask himself how, if labour produces goods to the value of only 20 milliards, they can be exchanged at a value of 25 milliards, and what is responsible for the increase of five milliards. The other contradictions which he brings forward are not indeed new, but they are ingeniously treated. For example : the essence of exchange-value is labour, which creates wealth ; but the more the wealth produced, the less becomes its exchange-value. Or this : the division of labour is, according to Smith, one of the most effective means of increasing wealth, but the further the division of labour proceeds the lower sinks the workman, being reduced to the level of an unintelligent automaton engaged in the performance of a fractional operation. The same thing holds good for machinery. So, too, competition stimulates effort, but brings much misery in its train by leading to adulteration, sharp practices, and strife between man and man. Further, taxation should be proportional to riches, in reality it is proportional to poverty. Or again, private ownership of land ought to increase productivity ; in practice it deprives the farmer of the land. In this way he runs to earth the contradictions in political economy, and so we find everywhere the words thesis and anti-thesis or antinomies (contradictions between two well-established propositions). And out of this contradiction springs poverty. The solution or the synthesis is the creation of an economic order which shall preserve the good elements in this category and eliminate the bad ones, and so satisfy the demands of justice. And that is what Socialism cannot do. " For the economic order is based upon calculations of an inexorable justice and not upon those angelic sentiments of brotherhood, sacrifice, and love which so many well-meaning Socialists of the present time are endeavouring to awake in the people. It is useless for them to preach, after the example of Jesus Christ, the necessity for sacrifice, and to set an example of it in their own lives : selfishness is stronger than they and can only be restrained by rigid justice and immutable economic law. Humanitarian enthusiasm may cause upheavals which are conducive to the progress of civilisation, but such emotional crises, like the fluctuations in value, simply result in the establishing of law and order on a more rigid and more restricted basis. Nature or the Deity planted mistrust in our hearts, having no faith in the love of man for his fellow men ; and though I say it to the shame of the human conscience (for our hypocrisy must be confronted with it sooner or later), every disclosure which science has made to us concerning the designs of providence with respect to the progress of society points to a deeply rooted hatred of mankind on God's part."—(" System of Economic Contradictions or the Philosophy of Poverty," Vol. I., p. 107.) Just as

severely does he denounce the institution of Trade
Unionism and its methods of warfare, together with
State politics, as indeed the working of class organisation and of the State generally.   The only way to
realise social justice is to create a society of producers
who   exchange   their   goods   among   one   another
according to their equivalents in labour and carry on
work in adequate relationship to the production of
wealth, or, to put it clearly, to establish an order
where supply and demand balance one another.

Marx's answer to the " Philosophy of Poverty "
is indicated at once by the title " The Poverty of
Philosophy." He deals first of all with the economic
details of Proudhon's work, and proves with docu-
mentary evidence that the theses and antitheses it
contains partly spring from a half-understood reading
of English and French political economists, and in
part have been taken direct from the English
Communists.   Marx already displays in this section
an extensive knowledge of economic literature.   Then
he confronts Proudhon's philosophical and social
theories with his own deductions and gives many
positive results.   Marx's main object was to induce
the Socialists to give up their Utopianism and think
in terms of realism, and to regard social and
economic *categories* in their historical setting :

" Economic *categories* are only the theoretical
expressions, ideal conceptions of the conditions of
production obtaining in society.   .   .   .   Proudhon
has grasped well enough that men manufacture cloth,
linen, etc., under certain conditions of production.
But what he has not grasped is that these social
conditions themselves are just as much human
products as cloth, linen, etc.   Social conditions are

intimately bound up with productive power. With the acquisition of new productive power men change their methods of production, and with the change in the methods of production, in the manner of obtaining a livelihood, they change their social conditions. The hand-mill gives rise to a society with feudal lords, the steam-mill to a society with industrial capitalists. But the same men who shape the social conditions in conformity with the material means of production, shape also the principles, the ideas, the *categories* in conformity with their social conditions. Consequently these ideas, these *categories*, are just as little eternal as are the conditions to which they give expression. They are the transitory and changing products of history. We are living in the midst of a continuous movement of growth in productive power, of destruction of existing social conditions, of formation of ideas."—(" Poverty of Philosophy," Stuttgart, 1885, pp. 100-101.)

Here it should, above all, be noticed that Marx ascribes to industrialism a powerful revolutionary effect, and that he characterises the different forms of society by their different methods of labour. Or, as he says later in " Capital," " not *what* is produced, but *how* it is produced distinguishes the various forms of society." What he means to say, then, is that ideas and systems are limited by their time, that they are conditioned by the prevailing means of production. To understand them one must study the times which have preceded them, as well as investigate the ideas and systems themselves, and find out whether new forms have not arisen which stand in contradiction or in contrast to the old one. Or, as Marx says :

" Feudalism, too, had its proletariat—the villeinage —which contains all the germs of the middle class. Feudal production, too, had two contradictory elements which are likewise characterised as the ' good ' and ' bad ' sides of feudalism without regard to the fact that it is always the ' bad ' side which triumphs ultimately over the ' good ' side. It is the bad side which calls into being the movement which makes history, in that it brings the struggle to a head. If, at the time of the supremacy of feudalism, the economists, in their enthusiasm for knightly virtues, for the beautiful harmony between rights and duties, for the patriarchal life of the towns, for the flourishing home industries in the country, for the development of industry organised in corporations, companies and guilds, in a word, for everything which forms the finer side of feudalism, had set themselves the problem of eliminating everything which could throw a shadow on this picture—serfdom, privileges, anarchy—where would it all have ended ? They would have destroyed every element which called forth strife, they would have nipped in the bud the development of the middle class. They would have set themselves the absurd problem of blotting out history.

When the middle class had come to the top, neither the good nor the bad side of feudalism come into question. The productive forces, which had been developed under feudalism through its agency, fell to its control. All old economic forms, the legal relations between private individuals, which corresponded to them, the political order, which was the official expression of the old society, were shattered."

Those Socialists and social revolutionaries who regard the hardships and struggles of society

as an absolute evil and plan the construction of a
society comprised solely of good elements, have not
grasped the meaning of the history of mankind. They
think abstractly. They misjudge both the past and
the present.

" Hence to form a correct judgment of production
under feudalism one must consider it a method of
production based upon contradiction. One must show
how wealth was produced within this contradiction,
how productive power developed contemporaneously
with the antagonism of classes, how one of these
classes, the bad side, the social evil, constantly
increased until the material conditions for its liberation were fully ripe.

" Does that not show clearly enough that the means
of production, the conditions under which productive
power is developed, are anything but eternal laws,
that they rather correspond to a definite stage in the
evolution of mankind and of its productive power,
and that a variation in the productive power of mankind necessarily brings about a variation in its
conditions of production ?

" The middle class begins with a proletariat, which
in its turn is itself a remnant of the feudal proletariat.
In the course of its historical development the middle
class necessarily develops its contradictory character,
which on its first appearance is more or less veiled,
existing only in a latent form. In proportion as the
middle class develops, there develops in its bosom a
new proletariat, a modern proletariat; and a struggle
arises between the proletarian class and the middle
class, a struggle which, before being felt, observed,
estimated, understood, acknowledged, and finally
openly proclaimed on both sides, issues in the mean-

while only in partial and transitory conflicts and acts of destruction."

In a special chapter Marx shows the necessity and the historical significance of the Trade Unions, which in spite of all the apprehensions and warnings of Utopians and Economists the workers have gone on establishing and perfecting, in order to be able to withstand the domination of capital. That means the gathering together of the divided interests and activities of the workers in a vast class movement, standing in opposition to the middle class; which, however, does not exclude the possibility of conflicting interests within the classes themselves, though these shall be put aside as soon as class is brought against class :

" From day to day it becomes clearer then that the conditions of production, among which the middle class moves, have not a simple, uniform character but one which involves conflicting elements; that the same conditions which produce wealth produce also poverty; that the same conditions which tend to the development of productive power develop also the power of repression; that these conditions only create bourgeois wealth, i.e., the wealth of the middle class, at the cost of the continued destruction of the wealth of individual members of this class and the creation of an ever-increasing proletariat."—(" Poverty of Philosophy," 1885, pp. 116-118, 177 sq.)

This antithetical character of capitalist society has for its effect that the political economists, who are the philosophers of the existing order, lose their bearings, while the Socialists, who are the philosophers of the proletariat, look round for means to relieve the distress. They condemn class struggles,* build Utopias and plan schemes of salvation, whereas the only real solution, because it is the only one which arises from the actual conditions, must be to further the organisation of the oppressed class and make it conscious of the objects of its struggles. For out of these struggles the new society will arise, and that, of course, can only happen when productive power has reached a high stage of development. Or as Marx himself proceeds :

" An oppressed class is a vital condition of any society founded upon class antagonism. The liberation of the oppressed class necessarily includes, therefore, the creation of a new society. In order that the oppressed class may be able to free itself, a stage must be reached in which the already acquired powers of production and the prevailing social institutions can no longer exist side by side. Of all the instruments of production, the greatest productive force is the revolutionary class itself. The organisation of the revolutionary elements as a class presupposes the existence in perfected form of all the productive forces that could in any way be developed in the bosom of the old society. Does this mean that after the collapse of the old order of society there will be a new class domination culminating in a new political power ? The condition of the emancipation of the working class is the abolition of all classes, as the condition of the emancipation of the third estate, of the middle class, was the abolition of all the three estates. The working class will, in the course of its evolution, replace the old middle-class society by an association

* The Socialists of those times were the Owenites and the Fouvierists, who condemned all class struggles, Trade Unionist strikes, and Labour politics.

excluding classes and their antagonism, and there will no longer be any real political power,* because it is just this political power which is the official expression of class antagonism within the community.

" Meanwhile the antagonism between proletariat and bourgeoisie is a struggle of class against class, a struggle which, when brought to its highest expression, means a complete revolution. And can one indeed be surprised that a society founded upon class antagonism should, at its final dissolution, issue in brutal conflict and collision of man against man? Let it not be said that the social movement excludes the political. There never was a political movement which was not at the same time a social movement.

" Only in an order of things where there are no classes and no class antagonism will social evolution cease to be political revolution. Until then the last word of social science on the eve of every general reconstruction of society must ever be : ' Fight or die ; bloody war or annihilation. Thus are we confronted with the inexorable question.'—(George Sand)."

With this battle-cry " The Poverty of Philosophy " comes to a close. It is the prologue to the " Communist Manifesto," which in itself is but a popular version of the positive doctrines developed in the controversy against Proudhon.

* Marx means the State.

III.

YEARS OF AGITATION AND VARYING FORTUNES.

I. THE REVOLUTIONARY SPIRIT OF THE FORTIES.

MARX was a revolutionary not only in the sense that he was the representative of a new conception of society and the founder of a theory of a new economic order, but also in the popular sense of advocating the use of force, in which connection he looked to the first years of the French Revolution as a model. He had a keen ear for the revolutionary rumblings in the depths of the populace. The years during which the elements of his new conception of society were accumulating in his mind and shaping themselves into a system were involved in a revolutionary atmosphere. In 1842 England witnessed the first strike on a large scale, which threatened to extend into a general strike and bore a political revolutionary character. In 1843 and 1844 the idea of the impending revolution was widely spread in England. Insurrections broke out among the Silesian weavers in 1844. In 1845 and 1846 Socialism spread rapidly on all sides in Germany, and Socialist periodicals appeared in the industrial centres. France swarmed with Socialist systems, Socialist novels and newspaper articles. The spectre of Communism was abroad in Europe. The convention of the United Assembly by Frederick William IV. at the beginning of February, 1847, was looked upon as the harbinger of the German Revolution. The connection between these phenomena could not escape acute intellects. Hand in hand with the extension of industry and the rapid construction of railways and telegraphs came alternations of economic prosperity and crisis, poverty grew, and the workers fought with ever-increasing bitterness against the iron law of wages and against the scanty pay, which hardly allowed the proletariat to eke out a bare subsistence. The cry in England was : " More factories, more poverty," but at the same time : " The greater the political rights of the masses, the surer becomes emancipation." Whoever lived in England and France during these years and had dealings with Socialism could not help feeling that political and social revolutions were on the march.

Already in his first letter to Ruge, written from Holland in March, 1848, Marx deals with the coming revolution, and foresees, to the astonishment of Ruge, who refused to believe it, that the Government of Frederick William IV. was drifting towards a revolution. At that time Marx had hardly begun his studies in Socialism ; and the further he advanced in these studies, elaborating his social dialectics and evolving the ideas of the class struggle, the more inevitably was he driven to the conclusion that the proletarian revolution, the seizure of political power by the proletariat, was the indispensable preliminary to the triumph of Communism.

Utopian Socialism stood outside the State and attempted to set up a Socialist Commonwealth apart from the State and behind the back of the State. Utopianism, with its moral and religious motives and mediæval Communist traditions, was pervaded with that spirit of contempt for the State which was char-acteristic of the Catholic Church during the period of its splendour. Moreover Marx, who recognised all practical forms of power, even if he did not always estimate them at their true value, saw in the State an executive power which it was a question of overturning and using as an extremely powerful instrument in the social revolution. As a result of his excursions into politics and French and English Socialism, Marx gave up Hegel's overstrained idea of the State and accepted the view current in Western European thought of the time; but he interpreted the State in the sense of the doctrine of the class struggle as the executive council of the ruling and possessing classes.

The impressions, the ideas, the experiences and the modes of thinking which took root in the mind of Marx during the evolution of the fundamental principles of his sociological and historical system dominated the whole of his life's work.

Marxism is quite a natural growth of the revolutionary soil of the first half of the nineteenth century. Marx completes the social revolutionary doctrines of that time, of which he is, as it were, the executor. All his thoughts and sentiments are deeply rooted in it; they have nothing specifically Jewish about them. I know of no Jewish philosopher, sociologist, or poet who had so little of the Jewish character as had Marx.

II. THE COMMUNIST MANIFESTO.

As in Paris, so too in Brussels, Marx frequented the society of German working men in order to instruct them by lectures and by conversation. He was loyally seconded by Engels, who had more time and more money to devote to this task, and who worked for the new doctrine in Paris, Cologne, Elberfeld and other towns. Since 1836 the German working men living abroad had been organised in the League of the Just, which from 1840 had its headquarters in London. The individual groups were kept in touch with one another by means of Communist correspondence committees. The Paris and Brussels groups drew the attention of the London Committee to Marx, and in January, 1847, Joseph Moll, one of its members, was commissioned to go to Brussels and obtain information about Marx. —(" Mehring's Introduction to the Reprint of the Cologne Communist Proceedings," published by *Vorwärts*, Berlin, 1914, pp. 10-11.) The result was the transformation of the League of the Just into the League of Communists, which held its first Congress in London in the summer of 1847, Engels and Wilhelm Wolf (Lupus) being among those present as delegates. At the second Congress, held in London towards the end of November and beginning of December, 1847, Marx also appeared, and together with Engels was commissioned to prepare a new program. The new program is the Communist Manifesto. Engels had come from Paris, Marx from Brussels. Before leaving Paris, Engels wrote a letter to Marx, dated November 24, in which he speaks as follows on the subject of the Manifesto :

" Just think over the confession of faith a little. I believe it will be best if we leave out the form of catechism and entitle the thing ' The Communist Manifesto.' And then, as more or less of it will consist in historical narrative, the present form is quite unsuitable. I am bringing along the manuscript which I have written; it is a plain narrative, but is badly put together, and has been done in a frightful hurry. I begin, ' What is Communism ? ' and then straight away with the proletariat—the history of its origin, difference from earlier workers, development of the antagonism of the proletariat and the middle class, crises, conclusions, with all kinds of secondary considerations thrown in, and lastly party politics of the Communists, as much as is good for the public to know."—(" Correspondence of Marx and Engels," Vol. I., p. 84.)

Engels' draft of the Communist Manifesto has been edited by Eduard Bernstein.—(" Grundsätze des Kommunismus," published by *Vorwärts*, 1914.) A comparison of this draft with the actual " Communist Manifesto " makes evident the full extent of Marx's intellectual superiority to Engels. The Communist Manifesto contains four main groups of ideas : (1) The history of the evolution of the middle class, its character, its positive and negative achievement—modern capitalism and the rise of the proletariat. (2) Theoretical conceptions and conclusions—the doctrine of the class struggle and the rôle of the proletariat. (3) Practical application—revolutionary action by the Communists. (4) Criticism of other Socialist schools. The last section has long ago lost all practical interest, so that we need only deal with the first three sections.

(1) The middle class developed in the bosom of feudal society, in the mediæval industrial towns. With the geographical discoveries of the sixteenth and

seventeenth centuries its sphere of activity was extended; it revolutionised the methods of industry, agriculture and communication; it broke through the mediæval economic and political bonds; it overthrew feudalism, the guilds, the little self-governing regions, absolute monarchy, and established modern industry with its accelerated and concentrated production, middle-class franchise, the national State, and, at the same time, international trade. It was the middle class which first showed what human activity can accomplish. "It has achieved greater miracles than the construction of Egyptian pyramids, Roman aqueducts, or Gothic cathedrals, it has carried out greater movements than the migration of peoples or the crusades. . . . Although it is scarcely a century since it came to be the dominating class, the middle class has created more powerful and more gigantic forces of production than all past generations put together." The subjugation of natural forces, machinery, the application of chemistry to industry and to agriculture, steamships, railways, electric telegraphs, the clearing of whole continents, making the rivers navigable, the conjuring forth of whole peoples out of the ground : that is the positive achievement of the middle class. Now for the negative : it created the proletariat, immeasurable, uncontrollable, anarchical economic conditions, periodical crises— poverty and famine in consequence of over-production and a glut of wealth, over-driving and reckless exploitation of the workers, whose labour is bought in exchange for the minimum quantity of the necessaries of life. These facts show that the forces of production are more extensive and more powerful than is demanded by the conditions under which they are operative : the economic system can produce and deliver more goods than society can use under the existing laws concerning property, i.e., the distribution and the effective demand fall short of the manufacture and the supply. The material forces of production press upon the limits imposed upon them by the laws of private property. This happens, too, because the working class must reduce its consumption of goods to a minimum in consequence of the existing laws of property, which give to capital the right of distribution. All these conditions taken together, the positive as well as the negative ones, make possible and give rise to the struggles of the workers against the middle class—and so the productive agents rise in rebellion. These struggles lead to the organisation of the workers in trade unions, to the awakening of class consciousness, and, as a result, to the formation of the political labour party.

(2) The movements within middle-class society, as well as in feudal and ancient society, where freeman and slave, patrician and plebeian, baron and serf, guild-master and journeyman, capitalist and working man stood and stand in constant antagonism to one another, prove that the whole history of mankind since the rise of private ownership is the history of class struggles, and that in these class struggles, carried on now openly, now under the surface, either new forms of society and of ownership, new economic systems arise or else end with the common destruction of the two classes. The antagonistic classes are supporters of conflicting economic interests, systems of ownership and ideals of culture. The craftsman and tradesman of the towns, the burgher, fought against the feudal lord and knight for individual

property, for freedom of industry and trade, for freedom to dispose of personal property and for the national State. With the triumphal progress of the middle class private property fell into fewer and fewer hands. The proletarians are without property, they have no share in the wealth of their country; on the other hand, the production of capital becomes more and more a matter of common co-operation, and capital becomes a joint product. The proletariat can, accordingly, no longer fight for individual ownership but for the socially conducted utilisation of the means of production belonging to the community and of the goods produced. The middle class has therefore created in the proletariat a social class which must have as its object to do away with the middle class system of ownership and to set up the proletarian system of common ownership.

(8) In this struggle of the working classes the Communists are therefore the pioneers of the movement. They are at once the philosophers and the self sacrificing champions of the proletariat awakened into class consciousness. " The Communists are not a special party in contradistinction to the other Labour parties. They have no interests apart from the interests of the whole proletariat. They set up no special principles according to which they wish to mould the proletarian movement." The Communists lay stress on the common interests of the whole proletariat and of the collective movement. Their aim is the organisation of the proletariat into a class, the overthrow of middle-class domination, and the conquest of political power by the proletariat. They support everywhere " any revolutionary movement against the existing social and political conditions.

In all these movements they emphasise the question of property, in whatever state of evolution it may appear, as the foundation of the movement. And finally the Communists work everywhere for the union and agreement of democratic parties* of all nationalities. The Communists disdain to conceal their views and intentions. They declare openly that their ends can only be attained by the forcible overthrow of every obtaining order of society. Let the ruling classes tremble before a Communist revolution; the workers have nothing to lose by it but their chains. They have the world to win. Workers of every land, unite ! "

From the standpoint of social philosophy, the Manifesto, a document reflecting its time, is almost perfect. Strong emotion and extraordinary intellectual power are united in it. Years of study of one of the boldest and most fertile minds are here welded together in the glowing heat of one of the most active of intellectual workshops. But the work is not free from logical flaws. In the passages we have quoted the part played in history by the middle class is extolled by Marx; yet in the last few lines of the very same section he declares that " the middle class is the unwitting and inert instrument of industrial progress," and still more scathing is his criticism in the second section, where the middle class is accused of indolence. " It has been objected that, if private property were done away with, all activity would cease and a general laziness set in. According to that, middle-class society would have been ruined by idleness long ago; for those of its members who work gain nothing, and those who gain do not work." That

* By democratic parties were then understood working-class political movements, such as Chartism, etc.

is as much as to say that the middle class is lazy and does not work, and yet the Manifesto says that the middle class has achieved more marvellous works than Egypt, Rome, and the Middle Ages, and that, in its reign of power of scarcely a hundred years, it has created more powerful and more gigantic forces of production than all past generations put together. How can a class which does not work produce more marvellous works than the whole ancient and mediæval world?

Marx frees himself later from this inconsistency by ascribing surplus value solely to the operation of the variable part of capital (wage-labour)—a doctrine which he develops with iron logic in his principal work, " Capital."

III. The Revolution of 1848.

The ink had hardly dried on the Communist Manifesto when the February Revolution broke out. The crowing of the Gallic cock soon awoke an echo in the various German States, whilst in Brussels the democrats were attacked and ill-treated by the mob. One of the victims of this attack was Karl Marx, who was, moreover, banished shortly afterwards by the Belgian Government. This action, however, did not cause him any embarrassment, as he was ready in any case to proceed to Paris, whither the Provisional Government of the French Republic had already invited him in the following terms :

" Paris, March 1, 1848.

" BRAVE AND FAITHFUL MARX,

" The soil of the French Republic is a place of refuge for all friends of freedom. Tyranny has banished you; France, the free, opens to you her gates—to you and to all who fight for the holy cause, the fraternal cause of every people. In this sense shall every officer of the French Government understand his duty. *Salut et Fraternité.*

FERDINAND FLOCON,
Member of the Provisional Government."

The stay in Paris was, however, of short duration. Marx and Engels gathered together the members of the League of Communists and procured them the means for returning to Germany to take part in the German revolution. They themselves travelled to the Rhineland and succeeded in getting the establishment of the newspaper planned in Cologne into their hands On the first of June, 1848, the *Neue Rheinische Zeitung* appeared for the first time. It goes without saying that the editor was Karl Marx, and among his collaborators were Engels, Freiligrath, Wilhelm Wolff, and Georg Weerth. Occasionally, too, Lassalle sent contributions. It is but rarely given to a daily paper to have such an editorial staff. In the third volume of his " Collected Papers of Marx and Engels," Franz Mehring gives a selection of the articles which appeared in this journal. They are still worth reading. Here are a few examples. After the fall of Vienna he wrote an article concluding with the following words : " With the victory of the ' Red Republic ' in Paris the armies from the inmost recesses of every land will be vomited forth upon the boundaries and over them, and the real strength of the combatants will clearly appear. Then we shall remember June and October, and we too shall cry, ' Woe to the vanquished ! ' The fruitless butcheries which have occurred since those June and October days .   .   . will convince the peoples that there is only one means of shortening, simplifying, and concentrating the torturing death agonies of society—only one means—revolutionary terrorism."—(*Neue Rheinische Zeitung*, November 6, 1848.)

Or take, for example, this passage from the last article of the paper, when on May 18, 1849, it succumbed to the " craft and cunning of the dirty West Kalmucks " (i.e., the Prussians).

" In taking leave of our readers we remind them of the words in our first January number : ' Revolutionary upheaval of the French working class, general war—that is the index for the year 1849. And already in the east a revolutionary army comprised of warriors of all nationalities stands confronting the old Europe represented by and in league with the Russian army, already from Paris looms the Red Republic.' "

In reading these extracts one has only to substitute Russia for France and Moscow for Paris and we get at one of the sources of Lenin's and Trotsky's revolutionary policy. The articles written by Marx in 1848 and 1849 have supplied the Bolsheviks their tactics.

The censorship, Press lawsuits, and the decline of the revolution severed the life threads of the paper after scarcely a year of its existence. Marx sacrificed everything he had in money and valuables—in all, 7,000 thalers—in order to satisfy creditors and to pay the contributors and printers. Then he travelled to Paris, where he witnessed not the triumph of the Red Republic but that of the counter-revolution. In July, 1849, he was banished by the French Government to the boggy country of Morbihan, in Brittany; he preferred, however, to go over to London, where he remained to the end of his life.

IV. DAYS OF CLOUD AND SUNSHINE IN LONDON.

Marx lived for more than a generation in London. Half of this time was spent in a wearying struggle for existence, which, however, did not prevent him from collecting and systematising a vast amount of material for his life-work, " Capital," nor from taking a decisive part in the Labour movement as soon as the opportunity presented itself, as it did on the founding of the International. The first decade was particularly trying. A letter written on May 20, 1851, by Marx's wife to Weydemeyer, in America, gives an affecting picture of their poverty during these first years of exile.—(" Neue Zeit," 25th year, Vol. II., pp. 18-21.)

The attempt to continue the *Neue Rheinische Zeitung* under the title *Neue Rheinische Revue* had only the negative result of swallowing up Marx's last resources. How poor Marx then was can be judged from the fact that he had to send his last coat to the pawnshop in order that he might buy paper for his pamphlet on the Cologne Communist trial (towards the end of 1852). On top of all this, lamentable differences sprang up among the German exiles,

who, deceived in their revolutionary illusions, over-
whelmed one another with recriminations; an echo
of these conflicts is heard in the pamphlet " Herr
Vogt " (1860). Marx's only regular source of income
in the years 1851—60 was his earnings as correspon-
dent of the *New York Tribune*, which paid him at the
rate of a sovereign per article, and this hardly covered
his rent and the cost of newspapers and postage. Yet
his articles were veritable essays, the fruit of researches
which cost him a good deal of time. And in the midst
of this penury the idea of writing a Socialistic criticism
of political economy burnt within him. One might
almost say that since 1845 this idea had allowed him
no peace. Freiligrath's lines are, as it were, stamped
upon him :

> In the clouds his goal he planted ;
>   In the dust had he to live,
> Bare existence daily granted.
> Cramped, hemmed in on every side,
>   Pinched by poverty and urged
> By want, he, of all denied,
>   By necessity was scourged.

Only in the sixties did his fortunes improve. Small
family inheritances, Wilhelm Wolff's legacy of over
£800, and Engels' more plentiful and regular help,
which from 1869 onward amounted to about £350
annually, enabled Marx to write his " Capital," the
first volume of which, as is well known, is dedicated
to Wilhelm Wolff.

To these relatively happy times belong Paul
Lafargue's reminiscences—(" Neue Zeit," 9th year,
Vol. I., pp. 10-17, 87-42)—of his intercourse with the

Marx family. In particular he depicts the personality of the author of " Capital." In the bosom of his family and among the circle of his friends on Sunday evenings Marx was a genial companion, full of wit and humour. " His dark black eyes sparkled with mirth and with a playful irony whenever he heard a witty remark or a prompt repartee." He was a tender, indulgent father, who never asserted the parental authority. His wife was his helper and companion in the truest sense of the word. She was four years older than he, and notwithstanding her aristocratic connections and in spite of the great hardships and persecutions which for years she had to suffer by the side of her husband, she never regretted having taken the step which linked her destiny with that of Marx. She possessed a cheerful, bright disposition and an unfailing tact, easily winning the esteem of every one of her husband's acquaintances, friends, and followers. " Heinrich Heine, the relentless satirist, feared Marx's scorn ; but he cherished the greatest admiration for the keen, sensitive mind of Marx's wife. Marx esteemed so highly the intelligence and the critical sense of his wife that he told me in 1866 he had submitted all his manuscripts to her and that he set a high value upon her judgment." Six children were born to the Marxes, four girls and two boys, of whom only three of the girls grew up—Jenny, who married Charles Longuet ; Laura, who became the wife of Paul Lafargue ; and the unhappy but highly-gifted Eleanor, who spent 14 sad years of her life by the side of Dr. Edward Aveling.

The sixties were undoubtedly the happiest years of Marx's life, and seemed to promise an abundant harvest in his later life. But his health soon began to fail, and did not allow him to complete his work. The most productive years of Marx's life were between 1887 and 1847 and between 1857 and 1871. All his valuable work falls within these years : the " Poverty of Philosophy," the Communist Manifesto, his activity in the International, " Capital," the Civil War in France (the Commune).

V. THE INTERNATIONAL.

The economic studies necessitated by his book " Capital " led Marx into the study of the social history of England during the eighteenth and nineteenth centuries, and gave him an insight into the working-class movements of those times such as but few scholars, English or foreign, have acquired. He became familiar with the modes of thought and expression of the working-class revolutionary movements, and especially of the Chartist movement, with the surviving leaders and adherents of which he was personally acquainted. Always eager to obtain knowledge of the actual working-class movement and to take part in it, he watched the activities of the English working class, which in the fifties was mainly occupied with purely trade unionist questions, being, politically, still in the Liberal camp. A change seemed imminent, however, about the beginning of the sixties. The London Labour leaders began to think about a Parliamentary reform movement, about starting a campaign for universal suffrage, which was an old Chartist demand. Likewise they manifested an interest in the fate of Poland and in other international questions concerning liberty.

At the International Exhibition held in London in 1862, the Labour leaders made the acquaintance of a deputation of French working men, with whom they afterwards carried on a correspondence. In 1863 and 1864, in the course of this correspondence, the idea of founding an international union of workers was mooted; and in the fourth week of September, 1864, this idea was carried into effect. Labour delegates from Paris and London held a conference in London from the 25th to the 28th of September, and the event was celebrated by a public gathering in St. Martin's Hall on the evening of the 28th. Marx received an invitation to this meeting in order that the German workers might be represented there. This conference and meeting resulted in the formation of the International Working Men's Association. Committees and sub-committees were elected to draw up a declaration of principles and outline the constitution. One of Mazzini's followers and a Frenchman submitted schemes which were handed over to Marx to be elaborated by him. He consigned them to the waste-paper basket and wrote the "Inaugural Address," giving a history of the English workers since the year 1825, and deducing the necessary conclusions. The declaration of principles is entirely the work of Marx, and it is by no means a subtly and diplomatically conceived composition designed to please English and French working men; it consists essentially of Marxian ideas expressed in terms, however, which would appeal to English working men of that time. " It was difficult," writes Marx to Engels—(" Correspondence," Vol.

III., p. 191)—" so to arrange matters that our view should appear in a form which would prove acceptable to the working-class movement with its present outlook. . . . It needs time before the re-animated movement will allow of the old boldness of speech. One must go *fortiter in re, suaviter in modo* (firmly maintaining essential principles with a pleasant manner)."

The Inaugural Address sums up the history of the English working class from 1825 to 1864, and shows that from its struggles, as indeed from modern social history in general, the following lessons may be learnt by the proletariat : independent economic and political action by the working class; the turning to account of reforms forced out of the ruling classes by the proletariat; international co-operation of workers in the Socialist revolution and against secret, militarist diplomacy.

Marx devoted a great deal of his time during the years 1865 to 1871 to the International. Its progress awoke in him the greatest hopes. In 1867 he writes to Engels : " Things are moving. And in the next revolution, which is perhaps nearer than it seems, we (i.e., you and I) have this powerful machinery *in our hands*."—(" Correspondence of Marx and Engels," Vol. III., p. 406.)

The International passed through three phases : from 1865 to 1867 the followers of Proudhon held sway; from 1868 to 1870 Marxism was in the ascendant; from 1871 to its collapse it was dominated and ultimately broken up by the Bakunists. The followers of Proudhon, like those of Bakunin, were against political action and in favour of the federative economic form of social organisation, only the

Bakunists were also Communists, whereas the followers of Proudhon had an antipathy to Communism. Both groups were in agreement with Marx only on the one point—that he made economics the basis of the working-class movement. Both groups, however, accused him of being dictatorial, of attempting to concentrate the whole power of the International in his own hands. Besides insurmountable theoretical differences, racial and national prejudices crept into the International as disintegrating factors. The Romance and Russian Anarchists looked upon Marx as a pan-German, and conversely, some Marxians considered Bakunin a pan-Slav. Even as late as 1914, in the first months of the war, Professor James Guillaume, the last of the Bakunists, wrote a pamphlet entitled " Karl Marx, Pangermaniste " (Paris).

Michael Bakunin (b. 1814, near Twer, in Russia; d. 1876, in Berne) lived and studied in Germany during the forties. In 1848 and 1849 he took part in the revolution, was arrested, then handed over to Russia and banished to Siberia, whence he escaped in 1856, afterwards living in various countries of Western Europe. He was an indifferent theorist, and contributed little to the enrichment of philosophical Anarchism, but he distinguished himself by his immense revolutionary activity and his capacity for sacrifice. The influence which he exercised sprang from his character. He had been acquainted with the Young Hegelians as well as with Marx, Engels, and Wilhelm Wolff since the beginning of the forties. Until the end of 1868 he acknowledged Marx as his intellectual leader, as is evident from the following letter which he addressed to Marx :

" 128, Montbrillant, Geneva,

" December 22, 1868.

" Serno has shown me the portion of your letter
which concerns me. You ask him whether I am
still your friend. Yes, more than ever, my dear
Marx, for now I understand better than ever how
truly right you are when you advance along the
high road of economic revolution and invite us to
follow, and when you set those below us who
stray into the side-tracks either of national or
exclusively political enterprises. I am now doing
the same thing that you have been doing for more
than twenty years. Since my solemn public leave-
taking from the bourgeois of the Berne Congress,
I no longer know any other society, any other
milieu, than the world of the workers. Henceforth
my country is the ' International,' of which you are
one of the most illustrious founders. You see, my
dear friend, that I am your disciple—and I am
proud of it. That will be enough to make clear
my   attitude   and   my   feelings   toward   you."
—(" Neue Zeit," 19th year, Vol. I., p. 6.)

Nevertheless, this discipleship did not hinder
Bakunin from secretly forming a separate organisation which contributed to the break-up of the
International. Moreover, the International was only
a kind of school for Socialist officers who had yet to
create their armies, but it proved even more successful than Marx himself could have expected. The
fundamental principles of Marxism ousted every other
social revolutionary system which had made itself
prominent within the working-class movement.

VI. THE PARIS COMMUNE.

On September 1, 1870, a part of the French Army was defeated near Sedan and compelled to capitulate on the following day. Among the prisoners was Louis Bonaparte, the French Emperor. The Empire fell on September 4, and France was proclaimed a Republic. On September 6 Marx wrote to Engels : " The French section of the International travelled from London to Paris in order to do foolish things in the name of the International. They want to over- throw the Provisional Government and set up a *Commune de Paris.*"—(" Correspondence," Vol. IV., p. 830).

Although the Provisional Government of the newly- baked French Republic was in no wise made up of friends of the democracy, Marx and Engels expressed themselves *against* any revolutionary action by the Paris working class. In the second Address (or declaration) of the General Council of the Inter- national, written on September 9, and composed by Marx, the question is discussed as follows :

" Thus the French working class finds itself placed in extremely difficult circumstances. Any attempt to overthrow the new Government, when the enemy is already knocking at the gates of Paris, would be a hopeless piece of folly. The French workers must do their duty as citizens; but they must not let themselves be overcome by the national reminiscences of 1792. . . . . They have not to repeat the past but to build the future. Let them quietly and with determination make the most of the republican freedom granted to them, in order to carry out thoroughly the organisation of their own class. That will give give them new, Herculean strength for the rebirth of France and for our common task—the emancipation of the proletariat."—(" Civil War in France," Second Address.)

Marx then urged the French workers not to do anything foolish, not to set up a revolutionary Commune of Paris, but to make use of their republican liberties to create proletarian organisations and to save and discipline their forces for future tasks. Circumstances, however, proved much stronger than any words of wisdom. Goaded by the anti-democratic moves of the Government supporters, deeply humiliated by the defeats of the French army, burning with patriotism and whipped up into fury against the " capitulards," the Paris working men cast Marx's words to the winds and rose in revolution on March 18, 1871, proclaiming the Paris Commune. Paris was to be the capital of a Socialist Republic. In seven weeks the Paris Revolution was overthrown —and " Vae victis ! " (Woe to the vanquished !) Marx afterwards wrote the pamphlet on " The Civil War in France, 1871," which is one of the most mature of his writings. He did not cut himself entirely adrift from the revolutionaries—the Bolsheviks of that time—but defended them with unsurpassable energy. It is the swan song of Marx and of the first International.

VII. The Evening of Life.

During the last twelve years of his life Marx had to fight almost uninterruptedly against various bodily ailments, all of which had their origin in his chronic liver complaint and over-exertion. His work, for which he had sacrificed, as he wrote to an American friend, " health, happiness and family," remained unfinished. He devoted his enforced leisure to making a study of American agriculture and of rural conditions in Russia, for which purpose he learnt Russian; he likewise occupied himself with studies of the Stock Exchange, banking, geology, physiology, and higher mathematics. In 1875 he wrote his " Criticism of the Gotha Program "—(" Neue Zeit," 9th year, Vol. I., No. 18)—which contains some very important data as to Marx's attitude to the State, to the revolutionary period of transition from Capitalism to Socialism, and lastly to Socialist society itself.

He went to Karlsbad for the purpose of recovering his health. In 1877 and 1878 he was in some measure capable of carrying on his work, and set about arranging his manuscripts and getting the second volume of " Capital " ready for the press; it soon appeared, however, that his capacity for work had gone. The decline in body and mind could no longer be checked; even visits to French and Algerian watering-places proved ineffective. It was just at this time that Marx began to find recognition both in France and in England : Jules Guesde, Henry M. Hyndman, Belfort Bax set about spreading Marxian doctrines, and Marxian and anti-Marxian parties were formed. But the man to whom this recognition had come was already a ruin. Bronchial catarrh, inflammation of the lungs, spasmodic asthma, together with the loss of his wife on December 2, 1881, and of his eldest daughter (Mme. Longuet) in

January, 1883, gave the finishing stroke to his
enfeebled body. On March 14, 1883, Marx breathed
his last. Engels gives an account of the last moments
in a letter to his American friend Sorge, dated March
15, 1883 :

" Yesterday, t half-past two in the afternoon,
the best time for visiting him, I went down to see
him.; everybody was in tears; it looked as if the
end had come. I made inquiries, trying to get at
the truth of the matter and to offer consolation.
There had been a slight hæmorrhage, but a sudden
collapse had supervened. Our good old Lena, who
had tended him better than any mother does her
child, went up, came down. He was half asleep,
she said ; I could go up. As we went in, he lay
there, sleeping, never to wake again. Pulse and
breathing had ceased. In those two minutes he had
gone painlessly and peacefully to sleep. . . . .
Mankind is less by a head, and indeed by the most
important head it had to-day. The working-class
movement will pursue its course, but its central
point, to which French, Russians, Americans, and
Germans turned of their own accord in decisive
moments, always to receive that clear, unambiguous
counsel which genius and perfect mastery alone can
give—is gone."

On Saturday, March 17, he was buried in the
Highgate Cemetery, London. Among those who spoke
at the graveside were Friedrich Engels and Wilhelm
Liebknecht. The former gave a brief account of his
revolutionary struggles, in which he said :

" Just as Darwin discovered the law of the evolution of organic nature, so Marx discovered the evolutionary law of human history—the simple fact, hitherto hidden under ideological overgrowths, that above all things men must eat, drink, dress, and find shelter before they can give themselves to politics, science, art, religion, or anything else, and that therefore the production of the material necessaries of life and the corresponding stage of economic evolution of a people or a period provides the foundation upon which the national institutions, legal systems, art, and even religious ideas of the people in question have been built, and upon which, therefore, their explanation must be based, a procedure the reverse of that which has hitherto been adopted. Marx discovered also the special law of motion for the modern capitalist mode of production and for the middle-class society which it begets. With the discovery of surplus value light was at once thrown upon a subject, all the earlier investigations of which, whether by middle-class economists or by Socialist critics, had been gropings in the dark. . . ."

After him spoke Liebknecht, who had hastened from Germany to pay a last tribute to his friend and master :

" The dead one, whose loss we mourn, was great in his love and in his hate. His hate sprang from his love. He had a great heart, as he had a great intellect. He has raised social democracy from a sect, from a school, to a party, which now already fights unconquered, and in the end will win the victory."

Engels, who outlived him by twelve years, edited the two last volumes of " Capital," while Karl Kautsky, the disciple and successor of Engels and the real disseminator of Marxian doctrines, edited the three volumes of Marx's historical studies on surplus value. The latter work is not far short of being a great history of political economy.

IV.

THE MARXIAN SYSTEM.

I. THE MATERIALIST CONCEPTION OF HISTORY.

A S a guide to his studies from 1843-4 onwards, Marx used the conception of history, or method of investigation, which—in contradistinction to the idealist conception of history of Hegel—was named materialistic. As its nature is dialectic—as it seeks to conceive in thought the evolving antagonisms of the social process—it is, like Hegel's dialectic, a conception of history and a method of investigation at the same time. Nowhere did Marx work out his method of investigation in a special and comprehensive form; the elements of it are scattered throughout his writings, particularly in the Communist Manifesto and in the " Poverty of Philosophy," and serve the purpose of polemics or demonstration. Only in the preface to his book, " On the Critique of Political Economy " (1859) did he devote two pages to a sketch of his conception of history, but in phraseology which is not always clear, sequential, or free from objection. It was the intention of Marx to write a work on Logic, where he would certainly have formulated clearly his materialistic dialectic. As, however, his fundamental ideas on this subject are available, we are able to extract the essentials of his position.

A glance over human history suffices to teach us that from age to age man has held to be true or false various opinions on rights, customs, religion, the

G

State, philosophy, land-holding, trade, industry, etc., that he has had various economic arrangements, and forms of the State and of society, and that he has gone through an endless series of struggles and wars and migrations. How has this complicated variety of human thought and action come about? Marx raises that question, which, so far as he is concerned, does not aim in the first place at the discovery of the origin of thought, of rights, of religion, of society, of trade, etc.; these he takes to be historically given. He is rather concerned to find out the causes, the impulses, or the springs which produce the changes and revolutions of the essentials and forms of the mental and social phenomena, or which create the tendencies thereto. In a sentence : What interested Marx here was not the *origin*, but the development and change of things—he is searching for the dynamic law of history.

Marx answered : The prime motive power of human society, which is responsible for the changes of human consciousness and thought, or which causes the various social institutions and conflicts to arise, does not originate, in the first place, from thought, from the Idea, from the world-reason or the world-spirit, but from the material conditions of life. The basis of human history is therefore material. The material conditions of life—that is, the manner in which men as social beings, with the aid of environing nature, and of their own in-dwelling physical and intellectual qualities, shape their material life, provide for their sustenance, and produce, distribute and exchange the necessary goods for the satisfaction of their needs.

Of all categories of material conditions of existence, the most important is production of the necessary means of life. And this is determined by the nature of the productive forces. These are of two kinds : inanimate and personal. The inanimate productive forces are : soil, water, climate, raw materials, tools and machines. The personal productive forces are : the labourers, the inventors, discoverers, engineers, and finally, the qualities of the race—the inherited capacities of specific groups of men, which facilitate work.

The foremost place among the productive forces belongs to the manual and mental labourers ; they are the real creators of exchange-value in capitalist society. The next place of importance is taken by modern technology, which is an eminently revolutionising force in society.—(" Capital " (German), Vol. I., Chapters 1, 12, 13 and 14, " Poverty of Philosophy " (German edition, 1885, pp. 100-101.)

So much for the conception " Productive Forces," which plays an important part with Marx. We come now to the other equally important notion, " Conditions of production." By this phrase Marx understands the legal and State forms, ordinances and laws, as well as the grouping of social classes and sections : thus, the social conditions which regulate property and determine the reciprocal human relations in which production is carried on. The conditions of production are the work of men in society. Just as men produce various material goods out of the materials and forces made available to them by Nature, so they create out of the reactions of the productive forces upon the mind definite social, political, and legal institutions, as well as systems of religion, morals, and philosophy.

" Men make their own history, but do not so spontaneously in conditions chosen by them, but on the contrary, in conditions which they have found ready to hand transmitted and given."—(Marx, " The Eighteenth Brumaire," I.)

That is to say, under the influence of productive work and its needs, men build their form of society, their State, their religion, their philosophy and science. The material production is the substructure or the groundwork, while the corresponding political, religious, and philosophical systems are the super-structure. And in such a manner that the super-structure corresponds to the foundation, lends it strength, and promotes its development.

The foundation is material, and the superstructure is the psychical reflex and effect.

In broad outlines this conception may be illustrated somewhat as follows :

Primitive human groups lived under Communism and were organised according to blood relationship. Their deities have the characteristics of their natural environment, and reflect the physical effects of this environment upon the primitive mental life of the " savage " ; their religion, their morality, and their laws promote the communal life and the tribal dis-cipline. Feudal society is based on the possession of land by the nobles and on the industrial labour of the corporations of the towns. The inherited religious ideas are soon transformed in accordance with the dominant interests of these historical periods (primi-tive Christianity became a State religion); all religious, ethical, and philosophical ideas antagonistic to these interests were fought and persecuted. The middle-class society, which is based on personal property, is endeavouring to sweep away all vestiges of communal and corporation rights, to set free the individual, to mobilise labour and property, to abolish Feudalism and the old Church and monasterial institutions, and to put in their place the individual relation between man and God, or the personal conscience (the Reformation), introducing individual rights as well; it struggles against the independent sovereignty of the feudal domains, and labours for a unified national territory, which will afford greater scope to trade and commerce; it supports Absolutism, so long as the latter is in conflict with the feudal lords; and when, afterwards, Absolutism is a hindrance to the development of middle-class society, this also is fought and a constitutional monarchy or a republic demanded. And all this takes place not because certain human intelligences, by reason of more intense thought, or enlightenment, or the call of a supernatural power, are primarily at work, but as a consequence of the influence of the material basis, of the economic foundation of society, upon the mind, which translates and transforms these external realities into religious, juridical, and philosophic conceptions :

" It is not the consciousness of men which determines their existence, but, on the contrary, their social existence determines their consciousness."— (Marx, Preface to " Critique of Political Economy.")

Man, even the most heroic, is not the sovereign maker and law-giver of social life, but its executive; he only follows out the tendencies and currents set up by the material foundation of society. Nevertheless, a great deal depends upon the executive officials. If they possess comprehensive knowledge, energetic natures, and outstanding capacities, they are able, within the boundaries drawn for them, to accomplish great things, and to accelerate the development.

" Up to the present the philosophers have but interpreted the world; it is, however, necessary to change it."—(Marx, " Theses to Feuerbach.")

We have referred in various places to interests. We are not to understand by this personal, but general social or class interests. Marx is not of the opinion that everybody acts in accordance with his personal welfare. This is not Marxian doctrine, but that of the middle-class moral philosophers, like Helvetius (1715—1771) and Jeremy Bentham (1748—1832), who regarded pleasure and pain of the individual as the measure and motive of his actions and conduct. Marx is rather of the opinion that men often, in the most important events of their lives, act contrary to their personal interests, as in their feelings and thoughts they identify themselves with that which they hold to be the interests of the community or of their class. According to Marx, individual interest generally plays a slight part in history. He is preoccupied with the collective interest of social production. Only the latter does he hold to be determining in the formation of the intellectual superstructure.

Up till now we have only spoken of various forms of production and society, and their corresponding mental systems. But we do not yet know why and how one form of production and society becomes obsolete and gives place to another, that is, how and why revolutionary changes are brought about. Or in other words : we have hitherto considered the statics of society ; we will now look at its dynamics.

The revolutionary changes in society depend on two groups of phenomena, which, although casually connected with each other, yet work differently. One of these groups of phenomena is technical, and consists in changes in the productive forces. The other group, which is the effect of the first, is of a personal nature, and consists in struggles between the social classes. Let us consider the first group of causes.

As the productive forces expand, through greater skill on the part of the worker, through discoveries of new raw material and markets, through the invention of new labour processes, tools and machines, and through the better organisation of trade and exchange, so that the material basis or the economic foundation of society is altered, then the old conditions of production cease to promote the interests of production. For the conditions of production : the former social classes, the former laws, State institutions, and intellectual systems were adapted to a state of the productive forces which is either in process of disappearing, or no longer exists. The social and intellectual superstructure no longer corresponds to the economic foundation. The productive forces and the conditions of production come into conflict with each other.

This conflict between the new reality and the old form, this conflict between new causes and the obsolete effects of bygone causes, begins gradually to influence the thoughts of men. Men commence to feel that they are confronted with a new external world, and that a new era has been opened.

Social divisions acquire a new significance : classes and sections which were formerly despised gain in social and economic power; classes which were formerly honoured decline. While this transformation of the social foundation is proceeding, the old religious, legal, philosophical, and political systems cling to their inherited positions, and insist on remaining, although they are obsolete and can no longer satisfy mental needs. For human thought is conservative : it follows external events slowly, just as our eye perceives the sun at a point which the sun has in reality already passed, as the rays require several minutes of time in order to strike our optic nerves. We may recall Hegel's fine metaphor : " The Owl of Minerva begins its flight only when twilight gathers." However late, it does begin. Great thinkers gradually arise, who explain the new situation, and create new ideas and trains of thought which correspond to the new situation. The human consciousness gives birth to anxious doubts and questionings, and then new truths ; leading to differences of opinion, disputes, strifes, schisms, class struggles, and revolutions.

In the next chapter we will consider more closely the class struggle between Labour and Capital. Meanwhile, we will look at the class struggle generally.

In primitive societies, where private property is yet unknown, or still undeveloped, there are no class distinctions, no class domination, and no class antagonisms. The chief, the medicine man, and the judge regulate or supervise the observance of the customary usages, religious ceremonies, and social arrangements. But as soon as the old order is dissolved, and private property develops, in consequence of trade with other peoples or through wars, there arise classes of those who possess and those who do not. The possessing class carries on the Government, makes laws, and creates institutions, which chiefly serve the end of protecting the interests of the possessing and ruling classes. The intellectual structure of the class society likewise corresponds to the interests of those who possess and rule. So long as these interests promote the common good in some measure, so long as the old forms of production and the old conditions of production are largely in harmony with each other, a certain truce prevails between the classes. But should there set in the above-mentioned opposition between the productive forces and the conditions of production, the latter will cease to satisfy the oppressed classes, and class conflicts will arise, which will either result in legal compromises (reforms) or will end in the overthrow of the society concerned, or will lead to a new set of conditions. Ancient history (Hebrew, Greek, Roman) is full of these social struggles; all the great reform laws of these peoples were attempts to establish social peace, but the rich and the poor, the Patricians and the Plebeians, the Slaves and Freemen, continued their struggles until the downfall of the old world, which has bequeathed to us great intellectual treasures as the fruit of these struggles. In the Middle Ages social struggles between the feudal lords and the traders, between nobles and peasants, were kindled. In more recent times the middle classes fought Autocracy and Squirearchy, and at length the proletariat was pitted against the bourgeoisie—class struggles which led to rebellions and revolutions, and powerfully influenced the intellectual life.

From these historical antagonisms and struggles arose the intellectual and political antagonisms, personified by the leaders of the social groups and

classes, of which world-history relates : opposing
religious and philosophical systems : Brahma and
Buddha, Baal and Jahveh, National God and
Universal God, Heathendom and Christendom,
Catholicism and Protestantism, Materialism and
Idealism, Realism and Nominalism. However
abstract or metaphysical, however remote from
actual life and material production they may appear
to be, nevertheless, in the last resort they are to be
traced back through many intermediate stages to
changes in the economic foundation of the society in
question, to the contradiction between this foundation
and the conditions of production, as well as to the
great struggles between conflicting interests which
spring therefrom. The ethical, political, and politico-
economic systems which strive with each other for
mastery, as well as national and world wars, are
separated from the real basis of society by a progres-
sively smaller number of intermediate stages : the
questions of idealist or utilitarian ethics, monarchy
or republic, oligarchy or democracy, protection or
free trade, State regulation or free scope for the
economic forces, Socialism or private enterprise,
etc., however lofty and humanitarian may be the
arguments and ideal motives which their champions
may adduce, are connected with the material foundation and the conditions of production which have
come into conflict with it.

Marx and Engels have set forth this conception in
the Communist Manifesto, in popular form, as
follows :

" Does it require deep intuition to comprehend
that man's ideas, views, and conceptions, in one

word, man's consciousness, changes with every change in the conditions of his material existence, in his social relations and in his social life?

" What else does the history of ideas prove than that intellectual production changes in character in proportion as material production is changed. The ruling ideas of each age have ever been the ideas of its ruling class.

" When people speak of ideas that revolutionise society they do but express the fact that within the old society the elements of a new one have been created, and that the dissolution of the old ideas keeps even pace with the dissolution of the old conditions of existence.

" When the ancient world was in its last throes the ancient religions were overcome by Christianity. When Christian ideas succumbed in the eighteenth century to rationalist ideas, feudal society fought its death-battle with the then revolutionary bourgeoisie. The ideas of religious liberty and freedom of conscience merely gave expression to the sway of free competition within the domain of knowledge."

Now one step farther. When the conditions of production, the social divisions into classes, and the laws of property become fetters to the productive forces, when the conflict of interests condense themselves into class struggles, then comes a period of social revolution.

" With the change of the economic foundation the entire immense superstructure is more or less rapidly transformed. In considering such transformations the distinction should always be made

between the material transformation of the economic
conditions of production which can be determined
with the precision of natural science, and the legal,
political, religious, æsthetic, or philosophic—in
short, ideological forms in which men become
conscious of this conflict and fight it out. Just as
our opinion of an individual is not based on what
he thinks of himself, so we are not able to judge of
such a period of transformation by its own
consciousness; on the contrary, this consciousness
must rather be explained from the contradictions
of material life, from the existing conflict between
the social forces of production and the conditions
of production."—(Preface to " Critique of Political
Economy.")

The revolutionary period only closes when the
social order that had become full of contradictions
liberates the productive forces and strikes off their
fetters, and creates new conditions of production which
correspond to them. The old society, which is doomed
to disappear, evolves the new conditions of existence
before it sinks into oblivion. The men who assist the
progress of the new society accordingly occupy
themselves with problems which they are able to
solve, as the means thereto are given in the material
development. Such problems are set before them
because, regarded from the theoretical standpoint,
they are the mental reflex of the contradictions and
revolutionary tendencies within society.

Accordingly, the essence of the historical development of human society has been so far the progressive
dialectical unfolding and perfection of the productive
forces.

" In broad outlines," says Marx, " we can designate the Asiatic, the ancient, the feudal, and the modern bourgeois methods of production, as so many epochs in the progress of the economic formation of society. The bourgeois relations of production are the last antagonistic form of the social process of production —antagonistic not in the sense of individual antagonism, but of one arising from conditions surrounding the life of individuals in society; at the same time the productive forces developing in the womb of bourgeois society create the material conditions for the solution of that antagonism. This social formation constitutes, therefore, the closing chapter of the prehistoric stage of human society."

Prehistoric stage of human society! What significant words! The capitalist economic order is the last phase of this stage, which is written in streams of blood and tears of the dispossessed and exploited, and to which is given the task of developing the productive forces and liberating men from the material fetters, so that they may enter into a life of mental culture. The materialist conception of history, unethical and unidealist like all natural science, opens up wide and elevating prospects. During thousands of years man struggled on the physical plane to obtain release from the animal kingdom, and was subjected to the discipline of unfeeling nature. After he had emerged from the animal kingdom, man laboured for thousands of years to lay the foundation of human society, a process which was performed under the hunger whip of stern taskmasters, and which powerfully stimulated the intellectual capacities of men, but only disclosed the ideal of justice and humanity as a remote and inaccessible star.

The materialist conception of history has shown itself to be a fruitful method of historical investigation. Some aspects of this idea were uttered both before and during Marx's lifetime. The revolution in the positions of classes and the struggles which followed hard on the English industrial revolution (1760—1825), and everywhere attended the transition from an agrarian to an industrial State, were too palpable to be overlooked. It was Marx who fused these ideas, with the aid of the Hegelian dialectics made of them a method of investigation, and pressed them into the service of Socialism and historical research.

II. CLASSES, CLASS STRUGGLES, AND CLASS-CONSCIOUSNESS.

One of the most important contributions of Marx to the understanding of historical processes is his conception of social classes and of class struggles. Although, prior to Marx, there were historians and politicians who pointed out the part played by social classes in politics and in social convulsions, it was Marx who first grasped this conception in its entire scope and significance, giving it precise form, and making it an essential part of political and social thought. He refers to the subject in the Communist Manifesto in the following terms :

" The Socialist and Communist systems properly so called, those of St. Simon, Fourier, Owen, and others, spring into existence in the early undeveloped

period of the struggle between proletariat and
bourgeoisie. The founders of these systems see,
indeed, the class antagonisms, as well as the action
of the decomposing elements in the prevailing form
of society. But the proletariat, as yet in its infancy,
offers to them the spectacle of a class without any
historical initiative or any independent political
movement."

The classification of the various groups of society,
or the division of human society into classes, is as
logical a process, that is, a result attained by the
operations of reason, as the division of animals, plants,
and minerals into various classes. A specific group
of social beings, which bear the stamp of common
characteristics, is put in a certain class by social
science. This classification cannot be made by purely
empirical methods of immediate sensuous perceptions.
It cannot be determined from the appearance of
modern men, whether they are capitalists or workers.
We must look for certain scientifically established
features which determine the social classification of
men. As we have just seen, Marx held economic
facts to be fundamental, and he contended that the
economic characteristics were valid for purposes of
classification. In his view, the manner in which a
specific human group obtained its sustenance was the
chief characteristic. Men whose chief means of life
are wages form the working class. Men whose
most important source of livelihood is the ownership
of capital (land, buildings, workshops, and raw
material) form the capitalist class. It is of little
moment that a worker owns a savings-bankbook, and
draws interest or dividends from a co-operative

society, or that a capitalist personally supervises his undertaking, or organises his business, so that his profits partly consist in wages of superintendence or salary. The outstanding feature is that the chief interest of the worker is concentrated on wages, whilst that of the capitalist is directed on property. It goes without saying that the social classes are not completely homogeneous. Like botanical and zoological classes, they may be divided into kinds and species; the working classes include well-paid hand and brain workers, as well as sweated sections; but all the subdivisions of the social classes possess the common outstanding quality of the same source of livelihood, which is either personal labour or the possession of capital. One class disposes only of labour-power, while the other class owns the means of production.

Between these two classes, says Marx, there are deep-seated, unbridgeable antagonisms, which lead to a class struggle. The antagonisms are primarily of an economic nature. The wage-earners, as the owners of labour power, are constrained to sell this as dear as possible, i.e., to obtain the highest possible wages, whereas the owners of capital endeavour to buy such labour-power as cheap as possible, i.e., to pay the least possible wages. This antagonism is indeed fundamental, but, at first sight, does not touch the intellectual sphere very deeply. On the surface, this antagonism is only one as between buyer and seller, but in reality the distinction is very great, as the seller of labour-power will quickly starve if he does not market his commodity. The owner of the means of production is therefore in a position to cause the seller of labour-power to starve, if the latter does not accept the conditions which the capitalist imposes.

Ownership of capital reveals itself as a power that can oppress the owner of labour-power.

This antagonism leads to the formation of Trade Unions. It is also the prime cause of the class struggle, but mere trade unionism is but its incipient stage. It develops into a class struggle when the workers recognise that their condition of subjection is not a temporary state, but the result of the economic system of private capitalism, that the subjection will last so long as this economic system exists, and that the latter could be replaced by an economic order in which the means of production belong to all the members of society. The wage-workers only participate in the class struggle when they learn to think in a Socialist sense, when hostility to the existing social order develops out of the sporadic and unrelated wage struggle and actions of Trade Unions, and when the proletariat, as an organised class, turns from the preoccupations of the present to the tasks of the future, and strives to change the basis of society from private property to common property. The workers then become aware that there can be neither freedom nor equality for them in the existing society, and that their emancipation can only be attained through Socialism. The class struggle may, however, stop short at the recognition of these facts. The dialectical movement will be incomplete if the working class does not take its fate into its own hands, and is not convinced that it has the power to achieve its own emancipation, and therefore contents itself with small social reforms, or relies on noble-minded and benevolent men and heroic redeemers. This was actually the case in the beginnings of the Socialist movement, when the workers saw in Socialism the only way out, but were still too weak to take their fate into their own hands. This was the period which Marx called Utopian, when outstanding personalities spread Socialist ideas, and made Socialist plans and experiments to free the labouring masses. As these personalities knew the impotence of the masses, they turned to philanthropists and humane rulers, and sought to convince them that reason, justice, and the general welfare demanded that Socialism should be introduced, and poverty, misery, and their consequences abolished. This period of Utopian Socialism gave way before the further development of industry, the progress of machine technique, the centralisation and concentration of the means of production and exchange, which brought with it an increase in the number, strength, organisation, and class-consciousness of the working classes. It is the centralisation of the means of production and exchange, in particular, which renders it possible for the working class, by paralysing industry and power stations, to cause the whole of society to feel that living labour-power forms the soul of the economic life.

At the same time Socialist investigators appear, who not only show the reasonableness and justice of Socialism, but exhibit the proof that the new economic order of Socialism is being prepared in the womb of Capitalism, and that therefore the aspirations of the worker are in harmony with the course of social development.

In this wise, a science and an aspiring Socialist movement founded upon reality develops from Utopian Socialism, and, conscious of class, of power, and of aim, enters upon the decisive struggle with the capitalist economic order. The class struggle acts as a lever of social revolution.

The original antagonism of the worker and capitalist over wages and hours of labour becomes an impassionate struggle of two classes over the question of the maintenance or transformation of the social and economic system—one of which classes fights for the existing order of private property and the other for the coming Socialistic system. Great social class struggles inevitably become political struggles. The immediate object of the struggle is the possession of the power of the State, with the aid of which the capitalist class endeavours to maintain its position, whilst the working class aims at the conquest of the power of the State in order to accomplish its larger objects.

The following chapter will show the direction taken by the Labour movement. Here we will but briefly refer to the profound influence of Marx's doctrine of the class struggle as exercised in political thought. Prior to Marx, political thought and the struggles of political parties seemed to revolve around ideas and great personalities. Idealogy and hero-worship were prevalent. Now, political thought, consciously or unconsciously, proceeds along class and economic lines. This is equally true of historical investigations. These new political and historical orientations are largely the result of Marx's life-work.

Rigidly conceived and applied, the Marxian doctrine of the class-struggle may lead to ultra-revolutionary tactics of the Socialist and Labour movement, to the system of Workers' Councils, and Proletarian Dictatorship. If the emerging class and its struggle constitutes the lever of social revolution and the

impulse of the dialectical social process, the Dictatorship of the Proletariat is justified, and in any case,
democracy, which includes both the capitalist and
working class, cannot be the State form during the
transition period from private property to Socialism.
Considered from the economic standpoint, political
democracy is generally impossible, or only sham
democracy so long as economic inequality exists.
The Communist Manifesto does not contain a single
political democratic reform. The conclusion can be
drawn from Marx's idea, as a whole, that in his
estimation, the class stood higher than so-called
democracy. This is one of the sources of Bolshevism.

III. The Role of the Labour Movement and the
Proletarian Dictatorship.

The Labour Party is the political expression of the
whole Trade Union movement so far as the latter
formulates national demands, directed towards the
State and society generally. The Labour Party will
function the more effectively, and be able to accomplish its allotted task, as its foundation—the Trade
Union movement—becomes established and strengthened, and the more comprehensive will be its
effects. The Trade Unions are not merely to be
satisfied with the work of the present, but are to
become the focus and centre of gravity of the proletarian aspirations which arise out of the social
transformation process, and are to work for the
abolition of Capitalism. The most effective lever for

the achievement of this object is the conquest of political power. With its aid the proletariat can consciously carry out the transformation of a Capitalist into a Communist society. To this transformation, there also corresponds a political transition period, the state of which can be nothing else than a revolutionary Dictatorship of the Proletariat.—(Marx, Letter to the German Social Democracy, 1875, on their Gotha Programme.)

Marx considered himself to be the real author of the idea of the Dictatorship of the Proletariat. In a letter written by him, in 1852, to his American friend, Weydemeyer, he declares :

" As far as 1 am concerned, I can't claim to have discovered the existence of classes in modern society or their strife against one another. Middle-class historians long ago described the evolution of the class struggles, and political economists showed the economic physiology of the classes. I have added as a new contribution the following propositions : (1) that the existence of classes is bound up with certain phases of material production; (2) that the class struggle leads necessarily to the Dictatorship of the Proletariat; (3) that this dictatorship is but the transition to the abolition of all classes and to the creation of a society of free and equal."— (" Neue Zeit," Vol. XXV., second part, p. 164.)

With the exception of the year 1870, Marx remained true to his doctrine of Proletarian Dictatorship : he thought in 1875 as he did in 1847, when he sketched the groundwork of the Proletarian Dictatorship in the Communist Manifesto :

" The first step in the revolution by the working class is to raise the proletariat to the position of ruling class, to win the battle of democracy.

" The proletariat will use its political supremacy to wrest, by degrees, all capital from the bourgeoisie, to centralise all instruments of production in the hands of the State, i.e., of the proletariat organised as the ruling class; and to increase the total of productive forces as rapidly as possible.

" Of course, in the beginning, this cannot be effected except by means of despotic inroads on the rights of property, and on the conditions of bourgeois production; by means of measures, therefore, which appear economically insufficient and untenable, but which, in the course of the movement, outstrip themselves, necessitate further inroads upon the old social order, and are unavoidable as a means of entirely revolutionising the mode of production."

But suppose that it is not the revolutionary working class which first attains to power in the revolution, but the democracy of the lower middle class and the social reformists. In this case, Marx gives the following advice : " Separate from it, and fight it." In the address to the League of Communists in 1850 he said :

" It may be taken for granted that in the bloody conflicts that are coming, as in the case of previous ones, the courage, resolution, and sacrifice of the workers will be the chief factor in the attainment of victory. As hitherto, so in this struggle, the mass of the lower middle class will maintain an attitude of delay, irresolution, and inactivity as long as possible, in order that, as soon as victory is assured, to arrogate it to themselves and call on the workers to remain quiet, return to work, avoid so-called excesses, and to exclude the proletariat from the fruits of victory. It is not in the power of the workers to hinder the lower middle classes from doing this, but it is within their power to render their success over the armed proletariat very difficult, to dictate to them such conditions that from the beginning the rule of the middle-class democrats is doomed to failure, and its later substitution by the rule of the proletariat is considerably facilitated.

" The workers must, during the conflict and immediately afterwards, as much as ever possible, oppose the compromises of the middle class, and compel the democrats to execute their present terrorist threats. They must aim at preventing the subsiding of the revolutionary excitement immediately after the victory. On the contrary, they must endeavour to maintain it as long as possible.

" Far from opposing so-called excesses, and making examples of hated individuals or public buildings to which hateful remembrances are attached, by sacrificing them to the popular rage, such examples must not only be tolerated, but their direction must even be taken in hand. During the struggle and after the struggle. the workers must seize every opportunity to present their own demands side by side with those of the middle-class democrats. The workers must demand guarantees as soon as the middle-class democrats propose to take the government in hand. If necessary, these guarantees must be exacted, and the new rulers must be compelled to make every possible promise and concession, which is the surest way to compromise them. The workers must size up the conditions in a cool and dispassionate fashion,

and manifest open distrust of the new Government,
in order to quench, as much as possible, the ardour
for the new order of things and the elation which
follows every successful street fight. Against the new
official Government, they must set up a revolutionary
workers' government, either in the form of local
committees, communal councils, or workers' clubs or
workers' committees, so that the democratic middle-
class government not only immediately loses its
support amongst the working classes, but from the
commencement finds itself supervised and threatened
by a jurisdiction, behind which stands the entire mass
of the working class. In a word : from the first
moment of victory the workers must no longer level
their distrust against the defeated reactionary party,
but direct it against their former allies, who would
seek to exploit the common victory for their own ends.
The workers must be armed and organised to enable
them to threaten energetic opposition to this party,
whose treason to the workers will commence in the
first hour of victory. The arming of the whole proletariat with rifles and ammunition must be carried
out at once, and steps taken to prevent the reviving
of the old militia, which would be directed against
the workers. But should this not be successful, the
workers must endeavour to organise themselves as an
independent guard, choosing their own chief and
general staff, with orders to support not the State
power, but the councils formed by the workers. Where
workers are employed in State service, they must arm
and organise in a special corps, with a chief chosen
by themselves, or form a part of the Proletarian
Guard. Under no pretext must they give up their
arms and equipment, and any attempt at disarma-

ment must be forcibly resisted. Destruction of the influence of the middle-class democrats over the workers, immediate independent and armed organisation of the workers, and the imposition of the most irksome and compromising conditions possible upon the rule of the bourgeois democracy, which is for the time unavoidable. . . . We have noted that the Democrats come to power in the next phase of the movement, and how they will be obliged to impose measures of a more or less Socialistic nature. It will be asked what contrary measures should be proposed by the workers. Naturally, in the beginning of the movement the workers cannot propose actual Communist measures, but they can (1) compel the Democrats to attack the old social order from as many sides as possible, disturb its regular course, and compromise themselves, and concentrate in the hands of the State as much as possible of the productive forces, means of transport, factories, railways, etc. (2) When the Democrats propose measures which are not revolutionary, but merely reformist, the workers must press them to the point of turning such measures into direct attacks on private property; thus, for example, if the small middle class propose to purchase the railways and factories the workers must demand that such railways and factories, being the property of the reactionaries, shall be simply confiscated by the State, without compensation. If the Democrats propose a proportional tax, the workers must demand a progressive tax; if the Democrats themselves declare for a moderate progressive tax, the workers must insist on a tax so steeply graduated as to cause the collapse of large fortunes; if the Democrats demand the regulation of the State debt, the workers must demand State bankruptcy. Thus the demands of the workers must everywhere be directed against the concessions and measures of the Democrats. . . . Further, the Democrats will either work directly for a Federal Republic, or, at least, if they cannot avoid the Republic one and indivisible, will seek to paralyse it by granting the greatest possible independence to the municipalities and provinces. The workers must set themselves against this plan, not only to secure the one and indivisible German Republic, but to concentrate as much power as possible in the hands of the State. They need not be misled by democratic platitudes about the freedom of the Communes, self-determination, etc. Their battle-cry must be ' the revolution in permanence.' "

This Address of Marx, written in 1850, appears to be the guide of the Bolsheviks and Spartacists.

The working classes may, however, not expect their immediate emancipation from their political victory.

" In order to work out their own emancipation, and with it that higher form of life which present-day society inevitably opposes, the protracted struggle must pass through a whole series of historical processes, in the course of which men and circumstances alike will be changed. They have no ideal to realise; they have only to set free the elements of the new society, which have already developed in the womb of the collapsing bourgeois society."—(Marx, " Civil War in France.")

The means of production will gradually be socialised, production will be placed on a co-operative basis, education will be combined with productive work, in order to transform the members of society into producers. So long as the transition period lasts the

Communist maxim, " From each according to his capacity, to each according to his needs," cannot become operative. For this period is in every respect —economic, social, and intellectual—still tainted with the marks of the old society, and " rights cannot transcend the economic structure of society, and the cultural development which it determines."—(Criticism of Gotha Program.) To each will be given according to his deeds.

" Accordingly the individual producer will receive back what he gives to society, after deductions for government, education, and other social charges. He will give society his individual quota of labour. For example : the social working day consists in the sum total of individual working days ; the individual labour time of the individual producer is the part of the social working day which he contributes ; his share thereof. He will receive from society a certificate that he has performed so much work (after deducting his work for social funds), and with this certificate he will draw from the social provision of articles of consumption as much as a similar quantity of labour costs. The same quantity of labour as he will give to society in one form he will receive back in another. . . The right of producers will be proportionate to the work they will perform : the equality will consist in the application of the same measure : labour."

Because performances will vary in accordance with unequal gifts and degrees of diligence, an unequal distribution will actually take place during the transition period. Only in a fully developed Communistic society, after the distinction between intellectual and physical labour has disappeared, when productive activity has become a first need of life, when the all-round development of the individual and the productive forces has been achieved, and all the springs of co-operative riches flow abundantly; only then can the narrow middle-class idea of rights be improved on, and the Communist principle of equality be put into operation.

Marx, who reasoned on strictly economic lines, and placed the emancipation of the working class as the highest goal, to which all other political and economic movements are subordinated, did not mistake the economic, political, and historical rôle of the nation : this is shown by the Communist Manifesto, where the creation of the national State by the bourgeoisie is indicated. He mocked at the young enthusiasts who thought they could brush aside the nation as an obsolete prejudice, but, in spite of this, he considerably under-estimated the unifying force of national feeling, considered from a biological and cultural point of view. He divided civilised mankind into antagonistic classes, and assumed that the economic dividing lines would prove to be more effective than national and political boundary lines. He was, therefore, through and through international. Marx demanded that the national Labour Parties should act internationally as soon as there was a possibility of the collapse of the capitalist domination. He reproached the original Gotha program with the fact that " it borrowed from middle-class Leagues of Peace and Freedom the phrase of the international brotherhood of peoples, whereas it was necessary to promote the international combination of the working classes in a common struggle against the ruling classes and their Governments." Marx had no confidence in the pacifism of the bourgeoisie.

IV. OUTLINES OF THE ECONOMIC DOCTRINES.

1. *Capital.*

As we already know, Marx became a Socialist in the year 1848. As a believer in dialectics, he knew that Socialism can only be understood by a knowledge of the movement operating in middle-class society and its developing forces. His investigations in 1843-4 led to the result that political economy forms the basis of bourgeois society. Henceforth political economy became the chief department of his studies. His comprehensive studies of French and English economists, especially Sismondi and Ricardo, and the anti-capitalist literature of England of the years 1820-40, which were connected with the Ricardian theory of value, furnished him with a wealth of suggestions and materials for the criticism of political economy, for the source and origin and development and decline of capitalism, written from the standpoint of the working class and the coming Socialistic society. Such a work is " Capital." It consists of three volumes. Only the first volume (1867) was carried through the press by Marx himself. The other two volumes he only sketched, and they were completed and published by Engels after Marx's death.

The first volume deals with the origin and tendencies of large industrial capital, with the immediate and simple process of commodity production, so far as it concerns the relations between employer and worker, the exploitation of the proletariat, wages and labour time, and the influence of modern technique on the condition of the worker. We see in the first volume the effect of the factory system in creating capital. Its chief figure is the producing, suffering, rebellious working class. In the second volume, the employer appears on the market, sells his commodities, and sets the wheels of production again in motion, so that commodities will continue to be produced. In the third volume, the realisation process of the undertakings of the capitalist class, or the movement of capital as a whole is exhibited : cost of production, cost price, total gains and their division into profit, interest and ground rent. The first volume presents the greatest difficulties. The tremendous efforts of the author to produce a masterpiece unnecessarily refined and sublimated and overloaded with learning the doctrines of value and surplus value until they attained the level of a philosophy, an example of Hegelian logic. He played with his subject like an intellectual athlete. That Marx could handle complicated economic questions in a clear, vigorous manner is shown by the third volume, which is written just as it came out of the author's head, and without the apparatus of learning subsequently erected, without the crutches of notes and polemico-philosophical excursions.

To understand " Capital " it is necessary to bear in mind that (1) Marx regarded the scientifically discovered principles as the real inner being of things, practice he regarded as the superficial appearance of things, capable of being apprehended empirically; for example, Value is the theoretical expression, Price the empirical; Surplus Value is the theoretical, and Profit the empirical expression; the appearances apprehended by experience (Price and Profit) deviate indeed from theory, but without the theory they cannot be understood; (2) he looked at the capitalist economic system as being essentially free from external hindrances and disturbances, free from invasions both by the State and the proletariat : the Labour struggles of factory protection laws of which Marx speaks in " Capital " serve rather to perfect the productive forces than to restrict the exploiting proclivities of sovereign capital.

2. *Value.*

The life and motion of capitalistic society appears as an infinite net of exchange operations, formed out of numerous entwined meshes.

Through the medium of money, men continually exchange the most varied commodities and services. A ceaseless buying and selling, an uninterrupted series of exchanges of things, and labour power—this constitutes the essential part of human relations in capitalistic society. An economic map of these relations, graphically displayed, would not be less confusing than an astronomical map which exhibited the manifold and intersected orbits of the heavenly bodies. And yet there must be some rule or law which operates in this seeming medley of movements ; for men do not work or exchange their goods by hazard, like savages who give their entire lumps of gold or rough diamonds for a necklace of glass pearls. The English and French economists in the seventeenth, eighteenth, and nineteenth centuries, amongst whom Petty (1628-87), Quesnay (1694-1759), Adam Smith (1723-96), and Ricardo (1772-1828) were the most original, sought for the laws which regulated exchange operations, and their theories were designated by Marx as classical bourgeois economy. Following up their investigations, Marx declared : Every commodity, that is, every thing or good produced under

Capitalism and brought to the market possesses a use value and an exchange value.

The use value is the utility of the commodity to satisfy a physical or mental need of its user : a commodity without use value is not exchangeable or saleable. As use values, commodities are materially different from each other; nobody will exchange a ton of wheat for a ton of wheat of the same kind, but he will for clothes.

In what measure will commodities exchange with one another? The measure is the exchange value, and this consists in the trouble and quantity of labour which the production of a commodity costs. Equal quantities of labour are exchanged with each other on the market. As exchange values, as the embodiment of human labour, commodities are essentially equal to each other, only quantitatively are they different, as different categories of commodities embody different quantities of labour. It is obvious that the quantities of labour will not be calculated according to the working methods of the individual producers, but according to the prevailing social working methods.

If, for example, hand-weaver A requires twenty hours for the production of a piece of cloth, which in a modern factory will be produced in five hours, the cloth of the hand-weaver does not therefore possess four-fold exchange value. If hand-weaver A demands of consumer B an equivalent of twenty working hours, B answers that a similar piece of cloth can be produced in five hours, and therefore it only represents an exchange value of five working hours. Thus, according to Marx, the exchange value of a commodity consists in the quantity of socially necessary labour power which its reproduction would require.

This quantity of labour is no constant factor. New inventions, improvements in labour processes, increase in the productivity of labour, etc., cause a diminution in the quantity of labour necessary for the reproduction of a commodity; its exchange value, or expressed in terms of money, its price, will therefore sink, provided that other things (demand, medium of exchange) remain equal.

Consequently, labour is the source of exchange value, and the latter is the principle which regulates exchange operations. Exchange value even measures the extent of the commodity wealth of society. Wealth may increase in volume, but decrease in value, in so far as a less quantity of socially necessary labour becomes necessary for its reproduction.

The more progressive a country is industrially and the higher the level of its civilisation, the greater is its wealth, and the smaller is the quantity of labour which must be expended on the creation of wealth. In the practical Labour politics of our times, this is expressed in higher wages and shorter working hours.

It was said above that use value is a basic condition for the exchange of the individual commodity. This does not exhaust the rôle of use value. The quantity of use value of which society has need determines the quantity of the exchange values to be created. If more commodities are required than society requires, the superfluous commodities have no exchange value, in spite of the labour that is expended on them. —(" Capital " (German), Vol. III., 1, pp. 175-176.)

The complete realisation of exchange values or the social labour that is performed depends, as is seen, on the adaptation of supply to demand, and is a matter of organisation, of social direction.

We have noticed that the Marxian theory of value is related to that of the classical economists, but they are by no means the same thing. Apart from some improvements and definitions which Marx made, they are distinguished by the following conceptions : In the classical theory of value, the capitalist who directs production and provides with his capital the tools and raw materials of labour, markets the finished commodity, and keeps going the processes of reproduction, appears as the only creator of value : the wage worker is only one of his means of production. In the Marxian theory of value, on the other hand, the wage worker who transforms the raw materials into commodities, or removes the raw materials to the place of production, appears as the sole creator of value. Value is only created by the worker in production, and in distribution connected therewith.

B. Wages and Labour.

The worker appears to receive wages for his work. In reality he receives wages as the equivalent for the labour power expended by him, quite in accordance with the law of value, inasmuch as he receives by way of exchange as much means of sustenance as is usual and customary to replace the labour power he has expended, just as the working horse receives as much oats and hay as are necessary to maintain it capable of work.

The capitalist and the worker exchange certain quantities of commodities in proportions determined by economic laws (means of subsistence against a quantity of the commodity, labour power, of equal value, commodity for commodity, exchange value for exchange value).

As, therefore, the wages of labour signify a certain quantity of the means of subsistence, so they increase even if their money form remains unaltered with a fall in the price of the means of life, for the worker is then in the position, with his unaltered wage, to buy a greater quantity of the means of life. In the reverse case, if the prices of the means of life rise, the wages of labour fall, even if their money form remains the same as previously. This law of wages, formulated by Ricardo, was accepted by Marx, but he did not content himself with this acceptance. Ricardo regarded the capitalist world as the only possible and reasonable one, at least at the time when he wrote his " Principles," while Marx from the year 1848 adopted a critical attitude towards it, and sought to negate it. Consequently, he investigated further, and expressed himself somewhat as follows :

The capitalist theoricians believed that the wages question was disposed of when it was settled by the law of value. We know, however, that every commodity possesses not only an exchange value, but also a use value, and is bought for the sake of the latter. The use value of the commodity labour power is distinguished in a very remarkable way from the use value of all other commodities.

The use or the employment of labour power creates exchange value, and can create much more exchange value than itself possesses.

The employer can make use of labour power so long that it not only creates its own exchange value (the value of the means of subsistence), but double this. To create the value of wages, the worker needs five or six hours daily, but he is obliged to produce for the capitalist during ten or twelve hours . If the worker were independent he would only produce during one half of the working day in order to receive his means of subsistence. This period of producing Marx called " necessary labour." As he is dependent on the capitalist, the worker must not only perform " necessary labour " but also surplus labour : the worker can generally only find employment under the conditions that, besides the time needed for himself, he also works a definite number of hours for the capitalist without payment. Or, as Marx says : " The fact that half a day's labour is necessary to keep the labourer alive during the 24 hours, does not in any way prevent him from working the whole day. Therefore, the value of labour power and the value which labour creates in the labour process are two entirely different magnitudes. And this difference in the two values was what the capitalist had in view when he was purchasing labour power. The circumstance that on the one hand the daily sustenance of labour power costs only half a day's labour, while on the other hand the very same labour power can work during a whole day ; that consequently the value which its use during one day creates is double what he pays for that use, this circumstance is, without doubt, a piece of good luck for the buyer, but by no means an injury to the seller."

" No injury to the seller," which is quite correct from the standpoint of Ricardo, but not from that of Marx. He often calls surplus value " unpaid labour," and says, for example, " the capitalist appropriates one half of every day's labour without payment." In other words, he takes away something without return. This is a very distinct ethical judgment.

On the other hand, it is very important that in our consideration of the wages question we have come up against the Marxian doctrine of surplus value. For this doctrine is the cornerstone of the whole economic system of Marx.

4. *Surplus Value.*

We have already noted that Marx followed the classical economics in his treatment of the theory of value, but improved the definition of it, and brought it to bear on wages. In doing this he laid stress on the conflict between Capital and Labour.

The beginning of this dialectical process, so far as England was concerned, was the work of the anti-capitalistic critics, who uttered their protest about 1820, or three years after the appearance of Ricardo's work. They declared, according to Ricardo, labour is the source and the measure of value. And yet according to his opinion labour is nothing and capital everything.

This should be reversed : labour must be all, and capital nothing. This literature was contemporaneous with the emergence of the English revolutionary Labour movement, from which Chartism arose at a later date. Piercy Ravenstone (1821) called capital a metaphysical (airy, impalpable) entity. Hodgskin (1827) called it a fetish, whereas they described labour as the economic reality. The expressions surplus-product and surplus-value were already known to this anti-capitalist school, with which Marx also connected himself when he set to work to elaborate his criticism of political economy.* But this literature supplied him with much less material for the construction of the theory of surplus value than the formulation of the theory of value of the classical economy. Besides,

* Compare M. Beer, " History of British Socialism," Vol. I., pp. 245—270.

while the English anti-capitalist critics, like Ravenstone, Gray, Hodgskin, and J. F. Bray merely condemned surplus value as immoral and as the source
of all social wrongs, Marx used the theory of surplus
value as the key to unlock the mechanism of the
capitalist system and to reveal its workings, its
tendencies, and its final destiny. This appears to be
the real difference between the English anti-capitalist
critics and Marx. In this matter he was obliged to
perform most of the work himself. The question he
put was no longer " What is the substance of wealth
and how is it measured? " but " How is its
growth and continual accretions to be explained? "
Capital is that portion of wealth which is employed
for the purpose of gain, of increase. Whence comes
this gain, this increase? The answer is as follows :

All capital that is embarked on a productive undertaking consists of two parts : one part is expended on
the technical means of production—on buildings,
machines, tools, and raw materials, the other on
wages. The first part Marx calls Constant Capital (c),
the other part Variable Capital (v). The first is called
constant, because it only adds to the commodities
just as much value as it loses in the course of the
productive process; it creates no fresh value : Marx
also calls it the passive portion. The outlay on wages
is called variable capital because it undergoes an
alteration in the process of production : it creates new
additional value : Marx also called variable capital
the active portion, for it creates surplus value(s).

This composition of capital of constant and variable
parts Marx calls its organic composition. He calls it
average or normal composition when the capital of
a business is 80 per cent. constant and 20 per cent.

variable. If the constant part is higher, and the variable part lower, he calls it capital of a high composition.

Capital of under 80 per cent. constant portion and over 20 per cent. variable portion he calls capital of a lower composition. And rightly, because the higher the ladder of capitalist production is, the more costly and extensive are the machinery and factory buildings and the greater is the outlay on raw materials, whereas primitive businesses employ less machinery, cheaper workshops, but a relatively greater number of workers. The relation between (c) and (v) reveals at the same time the stage to which production has developed.

Thus, according to Marx, it is solely the variable capital which creates surplus value, or, as it is commonly expressed, profit. We have seen above, in the explanation of the nature of wages, why variable capital creates more value than it is paid for by the capitalist; the worker does indeed receive the exchange value of his labour power, but the use value of the labour power functions, we have assumed, twice as many hours as are necessary for its reproduction. This surplus labour is embodied in surplus value. While the worker receives, let us say, a daily wage of three shillings, for the reproduction of which five hours of work suffice, his labour power will be used for ten hours. These five hours of surplus labour appear in the exchange value of the commodity, so that the value of the commodity is composed of the transferred portion of the constant capital, the outlay on wages, and the added surplus value. Immediately before the production process only constant and variable capital existed, or, in brief (c) and (v); after the completion of the production process, the commodity embodies constant and variable capital and also surplus value, or (c) and (v) and (s). This is the actual value of the commodity, (c) or, shortly expressed, c+v+s.

The relation between wages and surplus value, or between paid and unpaid labour, or, shortly, $\frac{s}{v}$, Marx calls the rate of surplus value : it expresses the degree of the exploitation of labour.

If wages amount to three shillings, which can be produced in five working hours, and if the worker works in the factory ten hours for these wages, so that he creates exchange value to the amount of six shillings, then the rate of surplus value is 100 per cent. The whole of the surplus value which arises in this manner in the process of production is called the mass of the surplus value, or shortly, m.s., that is to say, the individual rate of surplus value multiplied by the total number of workers engaged in an undertaking, or the total amount of wages.

5. Profit.

The mass of surplus value appears to the capitalist in the shape of profit. Surplus value is a Marxian scientific term which exactly expresses the principle of profit. Profit is a commercial expression which describes surplus value as it appears in practical life as a subject of experience, i.e., empirically.

The distinction between the Marxian theoretical and the commercial empirical conception is, however, not so simple : it arises from the different conceptions of the influence of capital and labour in the economic process. Let us explain it more distinctly.

As is known, Marx divided the capital embarked in industrial enterprise into two parts : into constant (technical means of production) and variable (living labour power, wages). He assumed that only the living labour power (wage labour) creates surplus value, whilst the constant capital only adds its own value to the new products.

The capitalist divides his capital outlay otherwise : into fixed (buildings and machines) and circulating (raw materials and wages) capital. The fixed capital is only used up slowly and only passes entirely into production during a series of years—let us say 15 years : thus of a fixed capital of £75,000, £5,000 would each year be consumed in the production of commodities, and written off in the balance sheet. On the other hand, the circulating capital (raw materials and wages) are wholly consumed in every period of production, and must be renewed at the beginning of a new period of production.

Suppose an industrial undertaking about to be started requires a capital expenditure of £105,000 : £75,000 fixed capital (for buildings and machinery), £20,000 for raw materials, £10,000 for wages. For convenience sake, we will suppose that the period of production lasts a year, and that the rate of surplus value amounts to 100 per cent., that is, the labour power receives a payment of £10,000, and produces a value of £20,000. At the end of the year, the capitalist reckons an expenditure of £5,000 on account of fixed capital, and £80,000 of circulating capital : the commodities produced cost, therefore, a net outlay of £85,000. This is the cost price, without adding profit. According to Marx, cost price signifies (c) and (v), therefore without (s), (surplus value).

But the capitalist knows that the manufactured commodities represent a greater value than the cost price. According to Marx, the surplus value amounts to £10,000 (as the variable capital of £10,000 creates surplus value at the rate of 100 per cent.); but the capitalist adds to the cost price a profit which includes the gains of the enterprise and interest on the capital outlay. If the capitalist were alone in the market, his profit might suck up the whole of the surplus value of £10,000; but he has to reckon with competition and the state of the market. The cost price, plus profit, is the production price as established by the capitalist. But according to Marx, that is, in pure theory, the production price is equal to the cost price, plus surplus value. There is thus a quantitative distinction—a difference in the amount of money—between the theoretical and practical production price, as well as a qualitative distinction between the notions of the capitalist and Marx respecting the source of profit. The capitalist believes that profit is the result of the portion of capital which he has put into the process of production, combined with his own commercial ability. On the other hand, Marx asserts that the capitalist can only extract a profit because the wage workers (the living labour power) create a surplus value in the process of production for which they receive no payment.

We assumed that the surplus value amounted to 100 per cent. measured with variable capital, and that £10,000 expended on wages produced £20,000. The annual balance sheet, however, would show the percentage of profit to the total outlay. Consequently, we must spread the £10,000 surplus value over the £85,000 which have been expended. The surplus value of an undertaking spread over the total capital

(c) Marx calls the rate of profit, or shortly, $\frac{s}{c} = \frac{10000}{35000} = 28.58$ per cent.

As a rule, the capitalist cannot sell under cost price without becoming bankrupt, but he can quite easily sell under the production price, and mostly does so. In the example already given, his rate of profit amounts to over 28 per cent. According to the degree of competition, or by reason of other circumstances which we will examine in the next chapter, he can content himself with a rate of profit of 10, 15, or 20 per cent., which will serve him partly as an income and partly be expended in the development of his enterprise. The 28 per cent. profit generally forms a circle within which he fixes his manufactured price. Under favourable circumstances he can add the whole 28 per cent. to the price; under less favourable, only 20, 15, or 10 per cent. Accordingly, several portions of surplus value remain in the commodities which are not yet realised. What happens to them? The remaining portions of profit or of surplus value fall to the large or small traders who are interposed between producer and consumer, or go in the form of interest to the banking institutions, in the event of the capitalist operating with borrowed money. As the profit is only realised in the process of circulation (in commerce and exchange) and there divided amongst the various economic classes and sections, most people believe that profit arises in commercial transactions. They do not know that the price of a commodity can only be increased in trade because its manufactured price was fixed below its price of production or its value, that is, because the commodities contain surplus value which is only gradually realised in the process of circulation.

The social significance of this doctrine is far-reaching. If it is correct, then all the social sections which are not engaged as manual and brain workers in the process of production, or in the transport of raw material, lead a parasitical life and consume the surplus value which is squeezed by the capitalist class out of the proletariat and appropriated without payment.

Quite otherwise are capitalist ideas. According to them, profit is the result both of the spirit of the enterprise and the ability of the capitalist, added to that portion of the capital which is put into the process of production : the machines and buildings and raw materials which are used up, and the labour power, all of which are bought at their proper exchange value. It is only fit and proper that the trader and moneylender should receive a portion of the profit so created, for they assist in realising the exchange value by bringing the commodities to the consumer, and thus rendering possible the process of production.

Surplus value or profit ? Labour or Capital ? Behind this question lurks the great class struggle of the modern social order. No wonder the Marxian doctrine of value and surplus value was the occasion for an extensive controversy, in which the famous problem of the average rate of profit played a great part.

6. *The Average Rate of Profit.*

According to Marx's doctrine of value and surplus value only variable capital creates fresh value and surplus value. An industrial undertaking of a lower organic composition, which thus employs much variable capital and little constant capital, must consequently create a greater surplus value or more profit than an industrial undertaking of higher composition which may employ the same total capital, but composed of greater constant and smaller variable portions than the former. Let us take two industrial capitals of £85,000 each. One expends £15,000 on the constant elements (machinery, raw materials) and £20,000 on the variable element (wages of labour). The other shows £20,000 constant part and £15,000 variable part. With an equal rate of surplus value—100 per cent.—the first capital would produce £20,000 surplus value (profit) and the other only £15,000 profit. Experience shows, however, that equal amounts of capital—in spite of temporary differences in profits—tend to produce equal profits. From this, it would appear that it is actually the capital expended and not the labour employed which determines the magnitude of the surplus value (profit), that the concrete results of the capitalist process of production do not confirm the Marxian theory of value, that the facts directly contradict the theory. It was Marx himself who drew attention to this problem. After he had constructed his theory of surplus value in the form of a scientific law, he continued : " This law clearly contradicts all experience based on appearance. Everyone knows that a cotton spinner, who, reckoning the percentage on the whole of his applied capital, employs much constant capital and little variable capital, does not, on account of this, pocket less profit or surplus value than a baker, who relatively sets in motion much variable and little constant capital."

How, then, can the equal rate of profit in the case of capitals of different organic composition be harmonised with the theory of surplus value ?

Marx concedes that equal capital sums whose organic parts are unequally employed give an equal rate of profit, although the volumes of surplus value created are different. Two capital sums of £50,000 each, one of which, for example, represents £40,000 constant and £10,000 variable capital, and with a rate of surplus value of 100 per cent. gives £10,000 surplus value, while the other is composed of £10,000 constant and £40,000 variable capital, and with an equal rate of surplus value gives an amount of £40,000 surplus value, will nevertheless yield an equal rate of profit, although theoretically they would be unequal if the rate of surplus value directly determined the rate of profit. In the first case, the rate of profit would amount to 20 per cent. and in the second to 80 per cent. In reality both undertakings yield an equal rate of profit.

How is this explained, according to Marx? By means of competition, the different rates of profit are levelled to a general rate of profit, which is the average of all the various rates of profit. Thus the capitalists do not realise the surplus value as it is created in any particular factory, but in the form of average rate of profit as it is produced by the operations of the total capital of society. The average rate of profit may be lower or higher than the individual rate of profit, for the " various capitalists," as Marx explains, " so far as profits are concerned, are so many stockholders in a stock company in which the shares of profits are uniformly divided for every 100 shares of capital, so that profits differ in the case of the individual capitalists only according to the amount of capital invested by each of them in the social enterprise, according to his investment in social production as a whole, according to his shares."

While thus the individual rates of profit do not proportionately coincide with the rates of surplus value, i.e., while the degree of exploitation of the worker in the individual factory, and the volume of surplus value thus individually created, do not directly determine the individual rate of profit, it is the total mass of social surplus value which is the source of the average rate of profit. If the mass of the surplus value be large, the average rate of profit will also be great. Marx says : " It is here just the same as with average rate of interest which a usurer makes who lends out various portions of his capital at different rates of interest. The level of his average rate depends entirely on how much of his capital he has lent at each of the different rates of interest." The higher the various individual rates of interest, the higher will be the average rate of interest at which his capital has been put out.

The individual price of production signifies, therefore, cost price plus the average rate of profit, and not plus surplus value : it does not necessarily correspond with the total amount of the constant and variable portions of capital employed in an individual enterprise, plus the mass of the surplus value : the prices and magnitudes of value of commodities are not manifestly equal, as Marx has often pointed out. Of course, the total profits of the capitalist class coincide with the total surplus value extracted from the working class, provided, of course, that the supply of commodities corresponds with the social needs.

Thus the law of surplus value, in spite of all deviations and refractions, holds good in the last resort. " In theory," observes Marx, " it is assumed that the laws of the capitalist mode of production develop freely. In reality, there is always only an approximation."

And the more capitalist production develops, the greater will be the degree of approximation in particular cases, for the progress of Capitalism signifies a continuous increase of constant capital, a more mechanical character being given to industrial processes, and a reduction of variable capital to the necessary minimum, so that the differences in the organic composition of capitalist undertakings become less, thus bringing the average rate of profit and the rate of surplus value nearer to each other.

This indirect and difficult method of realising profits involves the fact that the capitalist does not distinctly observe the exploitation of wage labour practised by him, but he believes that the profit is owing to his own commercial ability.

This difficult section of the outlines of the economic doctrines of Marx can be most fitly concluded by quoting the comprehensive observations of Marx himself upon this subject, which he gives at the end of his book.—(" Capital " (German), Vol. III., 2, pp. 855-6.)

" In a capitalist society, this surplus value or this surplus product (leaving aside accidental fluctuations in its distribution and considering only the regulating law of these fluctuations) is divided among the capitalists as a dividend in proportion to the percentage of the total social capital held by each. In this shape the surplus value appears as the average profit, which in its turn is separated into profits of enterprise and interest, and which in this way may fall into the hands of different kinds of capitalists. Just as the active capitalist squeezes surplus labour,

and with it surplus value in the form of profit out
of the worker, so the landlord in his turn squeezes
a portion of this surplus value from the capitalist in
the shape of rent. Hence when speaking of profit as
that portion of surplus value which falls to the share
of capital, we mean average profit. . . Profits of
capital (profits of enterprise plus interest) and ground
rent are merely particular constituents of surplus
value. . . If added together, these parts form the
sum of the social surplus value. A large part of profits
is immediately transformed into capital." In this
way, capital grows, or, as Marx says, accumulates.

7. *Surplus Value as Social Driving Force.*

It has been said already that capital is that portion
of wealth which is devoted to the object of increasing
wealth, of gain, the extraction of profit or surplus
value. This object dominates the capitalist class; the
desire for surplus value is the leading impulse and
principle motive of their activity. Goaded by this
desire and exclusively occupied with their special
interests, this class unconsciously and unintentionally
develops the entire capitalist system and leads it to
ever higher and more comprehensive stages.

Surplus value is thus the driving force of the history
of modern capitalist society. This principle is rigidly
followed out by Marx in his theoretical system, which
aims at showing the rise and growth of Capitalism.

The capitalist is no scientific investigator : he is not
clear himself whether profit is created by a portion
of the capital, or is the result of personal productive
forces, but he knows one thing—without living labour
power, without the wage worker, his whole capital
remains dead and does not increase; all the fixed

capital and raw materials are of no use to him so long
as they are not set in motion by living labour power
and transformed into commodities. His efforts are,
therefore, primarily directed to making proper use of
the living labour power. Historically considered,
little constant and relatively much variable capital was
employed in the primitive stage of the large scale
industry : there was as yet little machinery, and the
chief thing was the living labour power. The workers
were not yet factory proletarians in the modern sense,
but artisans who had lost their independent existence.

The capitalist harnessed them and utilised their
labour power and special ability. Consequently, he
strives to lengthen the working day, in order that as
many commodities and as much profit as possible may
be produced.

If previously the wage worker had laboured ten
hours, of which five were devoted to the production
of the value of his wages and five to surplus value,
he is now obliged to work for twelve hours, which
increases the period for surplus labour to seven hours.
The surplus value which is extracted through the
lengthening of the working day is called by Marx
" absolute surplus value."

Meanwhile, the capitalist learns by experience that
if the workers are so organised as to co-operate with
one another, the productivity of labour increases.
From this arises the mode of labour which Marx calls
Co-operation, or a reorganisation of the workplace,
which raises the entire production of commodities to
a higher level. The co-operation of the workers in
the process of production soon leads to the discovery
that, if the worker does not himself create the whole
product, but only a part thereof, he loses less time

and becomes quicker and more skilful in his work and produces more than previously. This discovery leads to the " division of labour," which indeed reduces the worker to the position of an automaton, or a living machine, but considerably augments commodity wealth. Division of labour again demands finer tools; mechanical problems arise to be solved by mechanicians and engineers. This favours the progress of mechanics. The growing commodity wealth, and the pressure to realise it profitably, renders necessary more extensive markets; the need for extension comes up against transport difficulties; transport problems arise, to be solved by road and canal engineers. The increasing variety of the labour process and the categories of commodities which are produced results in new metallurgical, physical, and chemical problems. Natural science flourishes.

Meanwhile, things are not so peaceful in the places of manufacture. The lengthening of labour time and the closer strain on their nerves and muscles, as well as the arrangement of the work, cause the workers to combine and struggle for improved conditions of labour. This struggle, together with the progress of natural science, of technology, and the expansion of markets, result in the discovery of machine technology, of steam and electricity, the foundation of large-scale industry.

The capitalist is impelled, on the one hand, to make himself as independent as possible of living labour-power; on the other hand, to increase the volume of his profits. The means thereto are offered him by the new technical discoveries. Those workers who still possessed some pride in handicraft, or as expropriated small peasants were not able to submit to factory discipline, and showed themselves rebellious, were partly replaced by the labour of women and children, and partly curbed and made pliable. The labour time is repeatedly lengthened, and the exploitation of the labour of women and children assumes terrible proportions. The wage worker, who entered into the manufacturing premises of the employer full of the pride of his calling and often with his own tools, became then a small cog in a gigantic, relentless piece of working machinery.

In this extensive and hitherto unprecedented social transformation the old forms of handicraft disappear : whole sections of society, which are the representatives of the disappearing forms of handicraft, sink into poverty, and augment the class of proletarians. The progress of the industrial revolution extends also to agriculture : the greed for surplus value (ground rent) leads to enclosure of common lands by the great landlords, the independent yeomanry is decimated, the small proprietor and small tenant are made proletarians. A transmutation of social classes takes place ; the urban population grows rapidly, the country districts are depopulated : out of the revolutionary process the outlines of two classes become more and more distinct : Capitalist and Proletarian.

Both the factory proletariat and the other social sections which adopt a hostile attitude towards Capitalism react against the health-destroying exploitation, and struggle for a normal working day.

The working time is curtailed and bounds are set to the efforts of the capitalist to lengthen the working day and obtain surplus value, but soon the progress of machine technique compels the worker to labour more intensely in the shorter working time : the accelerated movement of the machine determines the pace and necessitates a sharper straining of the nerves. Henceforth, the worker must compress into a working hour as much effort as was previously expended in an hour and a half. The surplus value which is extracted in this way Marx calls " relative surplus value." The struggle of the workers to secure a shorter working day is a powerful incentive to the manufacturers to perfect their machinery, in order to increase the amount of relative surplus value. The intensification of work or the creation of relative surplus value is one of the most immediate effects and one of the most striking features of advanced Capitalism. The understanding of this new phase is a preliminary condition to the comprehension of the Marxian system. In this matter, Marx goes considerably beyond the anti-capitalist theoreticians who followed upon Ricardo.

What happens when the capitalist observes that the extraction of absolute surplus value comes up against an insurmountable obstacle? He sets himself to fit up his enterprise with the newest and most costly machinery, in order to supplant living labour-power and to work more intensively the living labour-power which he employs.

As, however, less living labour-power brings forth less exchange value and less surplus value, he is obliged to multiply production, in order to cover the fall in surplus value by a larger mass of commodities : if the single commodity brings him less profit, he produces it in such large quantities that the profit thereon is the same, or even greater, than formerly. The more complicated machinery, the greater quantities of raw materials consumed, and the relatively

smaller amount of labour-power signify obviously an
alteration in the organic composition of capital : the
constant portion (machinery, raw materials) prepon-
derates more and more over the variable portion. If,
previously, the composition was 50 per cent. constant
and 50 per cent. variable, it becomes now something
like 80 per cent. : 20 per cent. At the same time,
the initial capital is also increased greatly, as machines
and large quantities of raw and auxiliary materials
demand such increase of capital. If, for example, the
initial capital previously amounted to £100,000,
divided into £50,000 constant and £50,000 variable
capital, it would now amount to £500,000, comprising
£400,000 constant and £100,000 variable. This
organic composition signifies : that relatively smaller
masses of labour set in motion large masses of technical means of production; labour is more productive
because more intense; the sum total of commodities
is increased; the profit on single articles is smaller,
but the total profit is greater; the reconversion of
profits into capital proceeds rapidly.

The scale of production is more and more extended,
and the amount of initial outlay becomes ever greater,
because only large capitals are capable of creating
relative surplus value in sufficient sums to assure a
profit on the enterprise and payment of interest, and
thus assist the accumulation of capital.

The more extended scale of production is not
possible to the less powerful capitalist undertakings.
They partly disappear and partly combine in joint
stock companies. The first alternative gives rise to
the concentration of the means of production in fewer
hands, and the second to the centralisation of the
means of production. This is the effect of the new

organic composition of capital on the capitalist class.

The effect on the working class is not less profound. As long as the hand-worker still played an important part in the works premises, as long as the variable part was superior or equal to the constant part in the organic composition of capital, as was the case prior to and at the beginning of large-scale industry, the accumulation of capital meant an increased demand for wage-labour. The position was changed as Capitalism developed, in the manner just described. Although the mass of capital grows, there is a relative decrease in the demand for workers. For this growth of capital refers chiefly to the constant part (machinery and raw materials), while there is a relative shrinkage in the variable part; that means the worker is obliged to consume a much greater quantity of raw material than formerly.

And whereas the prices of commodities fall during the phase of the high organic composition of capital, the period of necessary labour (the hours needed for the reproduction of wages) becomes shorter, while the period of surplus labour becomes longer. The great industrial development therefore signifies for the worker: intensive exploitation and relative over-population, a reserve army of labour-power, which is absorbed by industry in times of prosperous trade, and is speedily demobilised when the slump comes. In times of good business the reserve army serves to check the wage demands of the workers regularly employed, and in times of bad trade it serves to depress wages. The outcome for the workers is as follows :

" Within the capitalist system all methods for raising the social productiveness of labour are brought about at the cost of the individual labourer; all means for the development of production transform themselves into means of domination over, and exploitation of, the producers; they mutilate the labourer into a fragment of a man, degrade him to the level of an appendage to a machine, destroy every remnant of charm in his work, and turn it into a hated toil; they estrange from him the intellectual potentialities of the labour-process in the same proportion as science is incorporated in it as an independent power; they distort the conditions under which he works, subject him during the labour-process to a despotism the more hateful for its meanness; they transform his life-time into working-time, and drag his wife and child beneath the wheels of the Juggernaut of Capital. But all methods for the production of surplus value are at the same time methods of accumulation; and every extension of accumulation becomes again a means for the development of those methods. It follows, therefore, that in proportion as capital accumulates, the lot of the labourer, be his payment high or low, must grow worse. Accumulation of wealth at one pole is, therefore, at the same time accumulation of misery, agony of toil, slavery, ignorance, brutality, mental degradation at the opposite pole, i.e., on the side of the class that produces its own product in the form of capital."—(" Capital " (German), Vol. I., pp. 660-1.)

The result of the capitalist social order is the unfolding of the productive forces, the efflorescence of science, the expansion of material civilisation, the dividing of society into antagonistic classes, the conferring of economic power on the few, and the enslavement and degradation of the many.

8. *Economic Contradictions.* *Decay of Society and its Reconstruction.*

As the ripening of the capitalist social order to its highest point proceeds, its innate contradictions develop, and announce distinctly the fact that Capitalism has outlived its usefulness, while new life, a higher form of society, is emerging from its womb. The most important contradictions are :

The driving force of the capitalist is to obtain the largest measure of surplus value or profit. The latest stage of Capitalism is, however, marked by the fact of the high organic composition of capital, which means that living labour-power, the source of surplus value, has relatively decreased. The decrease of variable capital signifies manifestly a lower rate of profit. Capitalism in normal times exhibits a tendency towards a lowering of the rate of profit. Therefore it gives rise to a phenomenon which contradicts the aim of the endeavours of the capitalists. The capitalist strives to accumulate capital, but as variable capital and the rate of profit relatively decrease, a tendency towards the depreciation of capital is revealed. The capitalist endeavours to counteract this tendency, and to achieve his object by extending the scale of production, so that the mass of commodities will compensate him for what he loses on them singly. But while he furthers this object by resorting to a higher organic composition of capital, he squeezes out the middleman, reduces the numbers of workers in employment, and creates a relative over-population, a reserve of those who are only employed inter-mittently; there is a substantial shrinkage in the demand for commodities, as the impoverished masses of the people have obviously less purchasing power.

The capitalist extends production, and at the same time contracts the market. The upshot is over-production, under-consumption—crisis : wasting of capital, restriction of production, paralysis of the productive forces. And if Marx lived to-day he would add : the developed economy of large-scale capitalism, that is, the high organic composition of industrial capital, requires enormous quantities of raw materials, which, in part, are only to be had from tropical and sub-tropical countries, and also from eastern Asia ; the struggle for these sources of raw materials, and for access to them, leads to wars in which capital sums of unprecedented amount are destroyed. Since 1894 these wars over raw materials and trade routes have broken out every few years. Economic crises and imperialist wars ; immeasurable destruction of capital and productive forces. This is a consequence which stands in sharp contradiction to the historical task of the economic order of Capitalism, and to the immediate aims of the individual capitalists.

Further, the capitalist tries from the beginning to create docile and unresisting masses of workers, and yet unites and combines them by the creation of large centres of production ; the factories become centres for the organisation of the workers, and for the welding of the individual wills of the proletarians into a class will ; they abolish the scattered and antagonistic interests of single sections of the workers, and consolidate them into a unified class interest. Finally, the whole economic process, which began by resting on individualist principles, has assumed a common character ; thousands upon thousands of hand and brain workers engage in production in economic undertakings upon a single and uniform plan, with the aid of productive implements which can only be used in common.

The significance and tendency of these contradictions are sketched by Marx in the great finale, which properly belongs to the concluding chapter of the third volume :

" As soon as this process of transformation has sufficiently decomposed the old society from top to bottom, as soon as the labourers are turned into proletarians, their means of labour into capital, as soon as the capitalist means of production stands on its own feet, then the further socialisation of labour and further transformation of the land and other means of production into socially exploited, and therefore common means of production, as well as the further expropriation of private proprietors, takes a new form. That which is now to be expropriated is no longer the labourer working for himself, but the capitalist employing many labourers. This expropriation is accomplished by the action of the immanent laws of capitalist production itself, by the centralisation of capital. One capitalist always kills many. Hand in hand with this centralisation, or this expropriation of many capitalists by a few, develop on an ever-extending scale the co-operative form of the labour process, the conscious technical application of science, the methodical cultivation of the soil, the transformation of the instruments of labour into instruments of labour only usable in common, the economising of all means of production by their use as the means of production of combined, socialised labour, the entanglement of all peoples in the net of the world market, and with this, the international character of the capitalist regime. Along with the constantly diminishing number of the magnates of capital, who usurp and monopolise all advantages of this process of transformation, grows the mass of misery, oppression, slavery, degradation, exploitation; but with this, too, grows the revolt of the working class, a class always increasing in numbers, and disciplined, united, organised by the very mechanism of the process of capitalist production itself. The monopoly of capital becomes a fetter on the mode of production, which has sprung up and flourished along with it, and under it. Centralisation of the means of production and socialisation of labour at last reach a point where they become incompatible with their capitalist integument. This integument is burst asunder. The knell of capitalist private property sounds. The expropriators are expropriated."— (" Capital," Vol. I. English edition, chap. 84.)

CONCLUSION.

AN appreciation of Marx can only be arrived at by adopting the Marxian method. We must judge him in the same way as any other towering figure in the realm of thought or of action. Marx was a child of his time, and his system is a logical conception of certain economic and social phenomena of his age, owing something to the pioneer work and thinking of some of his predecessors.

Two important events dominated his thinking : the French Revolution and the English Industrial Revolution. Even apart from the statement of Arnold Ruge that in 1843-44 Marx had collected a vast amount of material for a history of the French National Convention, we know from the work he did between 1844 and 1852 how profound was the influence of the French Revolution on his intellectual life. Still deeper, however, were the traces left upon his mind by the studies he made on the economic transformation of England during the period 1760-1825. Both events are obvious, catastrophic expressions of class movements and class conflicts, in which the middle class, as the representative of a higher economic order, gains the victory over autocratic forms of feudal authority and oligarchic systems of organisation through State regulation, in which, however, at the same time, a new class—the working class—raises its head and begins to make a stand against the victor.

Marx was led to interpret these events in this way and to make them the basis of his conception of history chiefly through the influence of Hegel, Ricardo, and the English anti-capitalist school following upon Ricardo. To the end of his life he clung to the opinion that dialectic, as Hegel had formulated it, was indeed mystical but, when materialistically conceived, contains the laws of the movement of society. " The mystification which dialectic suffers in Hegel's hands in no wise hinders him from presenting in a comprehensive and intelligible manner its general processes."—(Preface to second German edition of " Capital," 1878.)

The splitting up of the concept into contradictories, and the attainment of a higher positive through the negation of these contradictories, that was what, to Marx's mind, constituted the essence and the deepest meaning of the French Revolution and of the English Industrial Revolution. Society, the positive, split up into feudal and bourgeois, into two sharply divided contradictories, the bourgeoisie appearing as the negation, to be supplanted by the proletariat and so to make room for a Communist society, the higher synthesis.

What he got from Hegel in a mystical form found an economic expression in Ricardo and the anti-capitalist school. Ricardo's writings, which belong to the second decade of the nineteenth century and which formulate, in the guise of a system of economics, the antagonisms and the conflicts between industry and landed nobility, presented themselves as a practical demonstration of the validity of dialectic. The fundamental idea of Ricardo's system may be expressed as follows :

Capital is the motive force of society and the creator of civilisation, but the fruits of its activity are enjoyed

not by capital but by the landed nobility. That is
the thesis; now for the proof. The value of all
commodities which can be made in any quantity
desired consists in the quantity of labour which is
expended for the purpose of producing them. The
value is expressed in the costs of production, the most
important components of which are wages and profit.
Wages and profit stand in opposition to one another :
if wages rise, profit falls, and conversely. Wages
consist in a definite quantity of the necessaries of life,
sufficient to keep the worker effective. Wages must
obviously rise whenever the cost of living rises. The
facts show that this is actually the case. The following reasons make this clear. In consequence of the
civilising effects of capital, there is an increase in the
opportunities for work and in population, resulting
in an increased demand for the necessaries of life.
Agriculture must be extended, but agricultural land
is limited and of varying quality. The extension of
agriculture brings into use the inferior kinds of land,
which demand a greater amount of labour for their
cultivation. And as the amount of labour determines
the value of the commodity, the cost of living
increases, and there is a rapid rise in ground rents.
The workers demand higher wages, whereby the
profits of the employers are diminished. But there
is still another circumstance to be taken into
consideration. Whereas the prices of agricultural
products rise, those of industrial products fall, since,
in consequence of the invention of machinery and
of the superior division of labour, smaller quantities
of labour are required to produce manufactured goods.
The result of the entire working of capital for the
civilised community is accordingly the reduction of

profits, the depreciation of capital, and the increase of wages. This latter, however, is of no advantage to the workers, for food prices rise higher and higher; on the contrary, the whole advantage falls to the landed nobility, who do nothing for the furtherance of civilisation, but who, through ground rents and protective tariffs, receive everything.

We have, then, in Ricardo a system of economic contradictions between profit, wages, and rent, or between bourgeoisie, proletariat, and nobility, in which the antagonism between bourgeoisie and proletariat is still undeveloped.

The year of the publication of Ricardo's " Principles " (1817) is the year which witnessed the rise of English Socialism. In that year, Robert Owen, in a public meeting in the City of London, declared himself a Socialist. Three years later appeared the first criticisms of Ricardo's political economy. In these it was argued that, according to Ricardo, labour is the source of value, yet he considers capital as the creative factor of society and the working class as a mere appendage of capital. It must be the reverse; for the workers create values together with the surplus products which are appropriated by capital. In 1817, Robert Owen openly declares himself a Socialist; four years later appears the anonymous letter to Lord John Russell; Percy Ravenstone publishes his " Criticism of Capitalism," John Gray his Lecture, and Hodgskin his pamphlet on the unproductive nature of capital, in which he establishes the existence of a raging class struggle.

The deep impression which these writings made on Marx is clearly seen in the second and third volumes of his " Theories on Surplus Value." And he links on to them. He completed what Ricardo hinted at and what the anti-capitalist school deduced from Ricardo. How Marx continued and elaborated these deductions we have already seen in Chapter 8, " Outlines of Marx's Economics," and Chapter 7, " Surplus Value as the Motive Force of Society," where capital is shown to be the mass of surplus value of which the workers have been deprived.

The deductions made by the English anti-capitalist school from Ricardo signified, politically, the first awakenings of the English workers to class-consciousness, to the struggle against capital. Just as Ricardo's theory of value and rent was the battle-cry of capital against the aristocracy—a battle-cry which created the free trade movement and shattered the economic power of the landed nobility, so the theory of value and surplus value was to become the battle-cry of the proletariat against the bourgeoisie, the declaration of independence, so to speak, of the working class. The English proletariat lacked a philosopher who could work out the idea to its logical conclusion, until Marx applied himself to the problem and solved it, so far indeed as philosophical problems can be solved, by a science which places itself at the disposal of a class movement.

For it is impossible to set aside the view that Marx's theory of value and surplus value has rather the significance of a political and social slogan than of an economic truth. It is for Marx the basis of the class struggle of the workers against the middle class, just as Ricardo's theory of rent was the basis of the class struggle of the bourgeoisie against the aristocracy, or as the doctrines of the social contract and of the natural rights of man formed the basis of the struggle of the middle classes against autocracy and divine right Such militant philosophies need not in themselves be true, only they must accord with the sentiments of the struggling mass. It is with such philosophical fictions that human history works. Marx's theory of value explains neither the vast and unparalleled accumulation of wealth nor the movement of prices during the last sixty years. Wealth, measured in values, has, in the last few decades, increased by many times the increase in living labour-power. In this connection the old formula can be reversed : wealth increases in geometrical, living labour-power in arithmetical progression. The greatest difficulty in Marx is that the inventors and discoverers, the chemists and physicists, the pioneers and organisers of industry and agriculture, are not regarded by him as creators of surplus values. Thinkers, who by chemical researches and discoveries double the productive capacity of the soil and conjure forth values in millions from the waste products of industry; physicists who place new sources of power and new means of production at the disposal of mankind and multiply the productivity of labour; organisers who co-ordinate the forces of production and introduce new methods of working—all this creative and directive work, demanding, as it often does, an infinite amount of intensive intellectual effort, is not considered to increase the total sum of exchange values of the nation.

However, as far as the distribution of products is concerned, Marx's theory is, generally speaking, correct; distribution is carried out under the capitalist economic system not according to the amount of productive work done, but in proportion to the outlay of capital and the skill in commercial manœuvring which obtains in the sphere of circulation.

Unique as an investigator of the laws of the proletarian movement, eminent and even a great pioneer as a sociologist, Marx is, in respect of economic theory, predominantly an agitator. His system, more than any other system of Socialism or of political economy, is the revolutionary expression of proletarian thought and feeling. His doctrines of value, surplus value, the economic determination of history, the evolution from Capitalism to Socialism, the political and economic class struggle, will for long have the force of truth for the masses and will continue to move them.

Marx's heart must have been filled with joy and gladness when, out of the elements of Hegel, Ricardo, and the English anti-capitalist school, out of his studies of the French Revolution, of the English Industrial Revolution, and of French and English Socialism there arose a unified system whose destiny it was to lead mankind out of the earth-bound history of the past into the new world wherein a spiritual civilisation should fully blossom forth. Man is to quit the realm of necessity and to enter into that of freedom, where he shall cease to be a tool for the profit of others and shall rise to have a purpose of his own, freely associating himself with his fellow men to work in the service of all.

" The realm of freedom, indeed, only begins there where work conditioned by necessity and external utility ceases. According to the nature of the thing, therefore, it lies beyond the sphere of actual material production. Just as the savage must struggle with nature for the satisfaction of his needs, for self-preservation and self-reproduction, so too must the civilised man, whatever be the form of society or the methods of production obtaining. Side by side with his own evolution develops this constitutional necessity, because his needs increase ; but, at the same time, the forces of production which satisfy these needs likewise increase. Freedom in this sphere can only consist in this—that men in their social relationship, the associated producers, should regulate this material exchange with Nature in a rational manner and bring it under their united control, instead of being governed by it as by some blind power; it should be carried on with the minimum expenditure of energy and under conditions most adapted to and most worthy of human nature. Yet it remains all the same a realm of necessity. It is beyond this where that development of human power, which may be called independent purpose, begins, the true realm of freedom, which, however, can only flourish upon the basis of that realm of necessity."—(" Capital," Vol. III., 2, p. 855.)

The National Labour Press, Ltd., Manchester and London. 31258

For Product Safety Concerns and Information please contact our EU
representative GPSR@taylorandfrancis.com
Taylor & Francis Verlag GmbH, Kaufingerstraße 24, 80331 München, Germany